RELEASED:
WALKING FROM BLAME AND
SHAME INTO WHOLENESS

A MEMOIR BY
PEGGY COOK

Front cover photograph by Peggy Cook
Back cover photograph by Carol Gates

EMPRESS
PUBLICATIONS
WWW.EMPRESSPUBLICATIONS.COM

Author's Note

My memoir is a writing of creative nonfiction.

I have changed the names of some characters.

I have used the real names of others only with their permission.

This memoir is not an indictment of any one religion or philosophy.

My writings are meant to illustrate how an individual needs agency in following their own truth. Using one's own voice, there are options to gain physical and mental health and wellness.

I wrote this memoir to give hope to those seeking a way to be comfortable and belong in this world.

It is never too late.

Peggy Cook
Newburyport, Massachusetts

DEDICATION

Do I have what it takes to make a difference?
Can I pass on my strength instead of my loss?
Edith Eger

To my mother, CHARLOTTE MARGARET COOK, who did just
that.

TABLE OF CONTENTS

PART VI: THE MOTHER

PART VII: EPILOGUE

PART VIII: END NOTES

INTRODUCTION

It didn't open easily.

I'd never inspected the bottom drawer in Mom's dresser. It was packed to the gills with gift-wrap and ribbon, nighties too pretty to wear, and half and whole slips she'd received as gifts.

Underneath these layers, I uncovered two baby books.

I had no idea I'd find pictures of Mom's two original Mother's Days by perusing this drawer. The first album had a black leather cover and jet-black pages bound with thick chord. The corners of each black-and-white photo were fastened with triangular corners.

This first was a book full of 4x6 prints of David's first days, weeks, and months. His first year as an only child. Infant David, lying in a blanketed wicker laundry basket broadly grinning, with Mom hovering over him. Mom in a plaid wool skirt and button-up cardigan. Her hair in a soft bun. Twenty-five years old. Daddy, holding toddler David, and Pop-Pop standing tall—three generations of Cook men in front of the family home in New Jersey. David, with his wispy blond hair, sitting on the hood of a Studebaker in front of Mom and Dad's first apartment in Boston.

Myriad photos labeled meticulously in Mom's handwriting. I feel Mom's excitement of first-time motherhood, just looking at what she'd put in David's baby book.

I slid the book back in its original hiding place under cover.

Next I lifted the lid off the white box, which sat next to David's book. This must be mine. I arrived four years after David. Thin tissue paper enclosed the book safely within the box. I lifted out the book, making sure I could rewrap it with the tissue creases exactly where they belonged.

"Our baby girl," printed on the cover, in pink, of course.

My heart pounded at this new evidence of my beginnings, four years after David's.

I opened the first page. A tiny square newspaper clipping fell out. "Baby girl born to Cooks." My grandparents must have sent it to Mom and Dad from the *Montclair Times* in New Jersey.

"A baby girl was born 1/23/50 to Charlotte M (Stachelhaus) Cook, and Theodore N. Cook, of Needham, MA. Grandparents, Gustav and Minna Stachelhaus, and Charles and Mildred Cook, reside in Upper Montclair, NJ.

The next page, nothing.

The next, still nothing. All pages wordless and pictureless.

My throat parched, I needed to swallow.

Not one photo, hair swatch, or comment.

That's what I got for continually searching for God knows what? I'd been looking for evidence of something since I was 8. Now I was 14.

I needed proof that I was celebrated despite my clubfeet. Proof of being a cherished infant, not just a burden and someone to constantly pray about. My birth, as a joyful event.

My face flushed as I stared at the evidence. I carefully folded the yellowed tissue and placed the book back in the box next to David's. I smoothed out the layer of Mom's clothing in the drawer, to make sure it could close, with no evidence of my hunt.

When Mom came home from the hairdresser that Saturday, I didn't let on that I'd been snooping upstairs. Or how stunned I was by my discovery.

PART I

THE CHILD

CAPTIVE

I understand what goes unresolved never loses its power.
—Honor Moore

I am at Norwood Hospital for my first clubfeet casting.

"Don't worry. We'll take good care of Margie."

My given name is Margaret. My parents call me Peggy, not Margie, with a hard *g*. I am only a year old. The frozen feeling of being called the wrong name by the nurse adds to my panic. I scream and writhe. She takes me from my mom.

I hear my mom crying and smell the Lysol in the dim corridor. That disinfectant smell goes up my nostrils into my memory bank.

The uniformed nurse carries me into a casting room in the basement of the hospital and lays me down on the stainless steel table, which is covered with a coarse white sheet. Two doctors stand ready for the procedure.

Voices echo, bouncing off the tiled walls. The bright lights mean business. In the 1950s a foul-smelling anesthetic, ether, is the way to put me out. A sieve, with a rag doused with ether, heads towards my nose.

I flail and whimper.

Surrounded by two doctors and a nurse, I lie flat on my back. The smell stuns and terrifies me. My throat tightens. I instinctively hold my breath. The nurse's voice echoes, "Breathe in, breathe in."

Finally giving in to the desperate feeling of suffocating, I have no choice and breathe in. Black and white circles swirl in front of my closed eyes.

While I'm asleep, the doctors manipulate my clubfeet and legs into the correct position. They are no longer crooked and deformed when held forcefully by the nurse. While she holds them firmly in that position, the doctors apply wet plaster from my feet to just below my knees. My casts hold that prayed-for position for the next eight weeks.

Then Dad carries me to the car. I'm semi-conscious. Still stunned, I drop my relieved head onto his shoulder. My mom sits in the back seat with me. She holds my plastery heavy legs in her lap. Dad covers me with a plaid blanket.

He drives slowly down Rt. 128 back home.

I spend the next two days resting and vomiting, lying on the living room couch. David, home from his overnight with a neighbor, stares at my casts. My head feels like a bowling ball, my legs like lead pipes. David sits on floor in his dungarees and t-shirt, watching *The Lone Ranger*.

I'm anchored to the couch while the plaster continues to dry. My mom holds a white enamel pot under my chin as I dry heave. When I need to use the bathroom, my dad carries me downstairs to the toilet and back to the couch.

I dream of pineapple juice, grape juice, and orange juice.

I am parched, but even small sips of water make my stomach churn, and soon I retch.

I long for toast. In a few days keeping that down is a sign of recovery.

In a day or so, my dad covers the cumbersome casts in dense white felt and tapes it on securely. The while adhesive tape stretches off the roll onto the casts.

When I can finally walk again, the felt prevents the plaster from cracking and digging into my feet. It gives me traction and keeps me from slipping on sidewalks or carpets. As the tape quickly becomes grass stained and filthy, my dad re-felts and retapes.

Mom shampoos my hair and gives me a sponge bath during these eight weeks in the kitchen. I dangle my head over the sink, lying on the counter.

Each casting day begins that same way. Those early morning surprises wake me, two times a year for the next five years, fall and spring. After the first time Mom and Dad appear holding my clothes so early, I know the routine. I scream and beg. No wonder my brother is having a sleepover at a friend's, although I never catch on to that obvious night-before hint.

"No, no, please, no, no." I scream all the way to the car. Now that I am older than 1, I have words, but they don't make a difference. I sob the whole drive to the hospital.

I am alone in the back seat of our Studebaker. By the time we arrive my throat feels like sandpaper and my head pounds.

Dad carries me into the dark hallway of the basement. We sit in the brown painted waiting room. No other family sits there this early. I sit on my mom's lap, while Dad keeps handing me little Golden Books.

I am not interested in *The Little Pokey Puppy* this morning.

The nurse arrives to take me to the casting. She reaches for my hand. I scream and plead to go home. My parents freeze.

I get it now. Why they can't console me. To them a hospital is a foreign place and "enemy" territory. I am supposed to be healed by God. They are speechless at this horrifying turn of events.

"I have to go to the bathroom, I have to go to the bathroom," I wail.

The nurse allows this brief reprieve. Mom walks me down to the bathroom adjoining the casting room. The nurse follows.

I plead some more. Sitting on the toilet in a panic, I beg. "Please, please, I'll be good."

Mom ignores my voice and sings hymns while I sit there. "Oh, gentle presence, peace and joy and power." That's my favorite hymn at bedtime. But not here.

Coming out of the bathroom way too soon for me, the nurse lifts me onto the table. Mom slides out of the room. I am deserted, abandoned to these strange people in white.

My mom dreamed of a ballerina daughter. Instead her daughter needs her legs and feet straightened by a doctor. I get it. They can't bear to warn me the night before. Knowing how high-strung I am, my parents choose secrecy, and these twice-yearly visits to Norwood Hospital define my early childhood.

I get lots of praise for "just going right on doing what you always do." I ride my tricycle, getting used to the thick casts on each pedal. On the green jungle gym in our back yard, I hang upside down. My cautious mom tells me later she had to look away.

I might look daring, but I feel unsafe and frightened most of the time. Something always looms right around the corner. Only Mom and Dad know when.

When it is time for my casts to come off, I behave like a different child. I don't mind driving into the Norwood Hospital parking lot. I look forward to my imminent freedom. I don't mind being lifted onto the table in the casting room. The noise of the saw doesn't scare me.

My appointment is on the calendar for weeks, and I look forward to it. I choose a skirt for the unveiling.

The doctor first shows me on my fingernail how the saw cuts without injuring. Then I feel the itchy sensation as the saw cuts through the plaster of each cast. The doctor carefully cracks the casts in half and my white shriveled feet and legs emerge straight as arrows. The nurse washes my ticklish feet and legs. Then she wraps each foot and leg in an ace bandage for support. My clunky casts land in the trash in the casting room.

My feet don't feel attached to me since the casts have been on for eight weeks. But my mom brings along little red leather slippers with plaid lining. She lifts me off the table. My stiff feet walk straight, but haltingly, in those slippers. I walk out the double doors to the car of my mom's best friend. Mom doesn't drive yet.

I wait by the front door for my dad to come home from work. I'm proud of my straight feet and new red slippers. We all go out for Brigham's ice cream.

My dad stretches my feet each morning to get my "heel" down on the ground again, so I can walk flat. His hands feel gentle and warm. He keeps my feet supple for as long as he can.

We have a few pictures of me with party shoes on just after casting. I grin with my feet facing forward, not a clubfoot captive anymore.

But in a few weeks my feet "relapse" back into the clubfoot position. The photos show me wincing and looking away again. Cameras never lie. After I turn 5, my parents stop getting my feet casted. Dad tells me I become too upset and make a "scene" during casting.

Much, much later, reading about childhood trauma, I start to understand the underpinnings of my childhood behavior. Always hyper-alert, traumatized from being held down and left alone, for so long I don't want anyone to touch me. I can't give or receive hugs without wincing. "Don't come close," my entire body warns. I can't look people in the eye. I am perpetually afraid what might happen next. My trust is destroyed by unwelcome surprises.

For so long, I tiptoe around like a skittish animal.

PEGGY'S HAVING TROUBLE

*Don't tell me what I'm feeling...You can die more than once in your life,
you know.*

James Hillman

I pull my blankets right up to my chin. I reposition Gray Kitty to make sure she is right under my left armpit, as close as she can get. I feel her wooly warmth and I finger her smooth glass eyes. The door shut tight, the room black. The cloth window shades down. The windows are open a crack for air.

David lies in bed way across the room. He might be asleep already.

I hunker down as close to the wall as I can with kitty. Then I wake with a start. My panic comes from somewhere familiar. Do I see shadows on the wall, even with the shades down?

Do I hear the fire horn blaring its cry for the engines to come quickly? Is the fire near us?

"I have to go to the bathroom." I sing out across the dark room. "I have to go to the bathroom." My notes become higher, the words faster, as no one responds. "I have to go to the bathroom!" My voice is shrill, hoping someone "saves" me.

David lends his voice. "Peggy's having trouble." Slowly, calmly. One more time a bit louder. "Peggy's having trouble."

Finally the door opens. I see a crack of light from the hall. In the corner of my twin bed I still clutch kitty. She has no tail. I am so close to the wall, I might fall through to the floor.

Mom whispers, "God is with you." She is standing next to the side of my bed.

I recognize her bathrobe smell of baby powder.

How does she know I don't need to go the bathroom? Why doesn't she offer to take me downstairs? How does she know I'm not "having trouble?"

There's plenty of room in my twin bed for her to come lie down with me. She keeps standing over me. I wish her hands would reach out to pick me up. I don't weigh too much. I'm just 3 years old. But she keeps standing over me.

Lie down with me, lie down with me, I pray.

She knows me well. She knows I don't have to go to the bathroom. David and I know how to send secret coded messages. We know their meanings. "Peggy seems scared to death again about something and needs you."

Mom knows I only need God. So she tells me God is always with me.

Kitty feels lumpy under my armpit.

Mom walks out of the vast bedroom in her pink bathrobe and beaded slippers.

She thinks all is well. That's why Dad doesn't come in. He knows God's care for me is ever-present. But I'm still scared.

SILENCED

...that type of absolute authority has always rankled me. But I listened to it for a long time.

Maureen Murdock

Nail biting always helps me take command of my body. I'm not quite sure when the habit starts, maybe when I'm 5 or 6. When I rip off my fingernails, they grow back. I have proof I'm alive and have a body. I often doubt I'm a person like everyone else. I am an observer of my own discomfort. "Discomfort" sounds less real than pain. I'm learning to "unsee" pain.

As I begin puberty, I look in the bathroom mirror each morning, trying to distance myself from that imperfect image looking at me. I stare at that body. It lives alone, empty. It's my painful shell I cannot fully desert. It's my enemy that doesn't answer commands, and yet, an ally that tries its best.

When I need to walk, I move back into my body to give it commands. My back and hips ache from the torquing to keep from falling. I compensate for the inward direction of my feet and knees with every step. The cobbler adds wedges to my ugly tie shoes to keep my feet from rolling over as I walk. They don't help with the pulling I feel in the back of my legs every day.

So I bite my fingernails to the nub. I feel shooting pain as I get too close to the cuticle. Why does my family say pain is a lie about man?

From a young age I learn: "Take possession of your body, and govern its feeling and action.... God has made man capable of this...." I memorize this religious text as Sunday school homework. But I'm not capable at all. I'm alone in my reality, pondering my appendages.

My parents stare at me. Maybe not. They are expecting me to understand enough about God's power. I can't. Sometimes Dad gets frustrated and accuses me of "not being receptive to the truth." But, to me, God holds court like the tooth fairy, which we aren't allowed to believe in. Only the truth. No Santa, no Easter Bunny, but an invisible God that can heal deformed bones. I don't get how this works.

One of the hymns Mom sings to me every night says, "I will listen for Thy voice, lest my footsteps stray."

But my feet stray continually. Perhaps I'm too literal.

I do hear voices though. Not God's voice. The voices I hear say, *You're ugly.* They say, *Everyone can see the weird way you walk.* Human encounters loom large to me. I could be obliterated at any moment by a nasty comment or a stare following me down the street.

I believe these negative voices. They sound accurate. I have eyes. I keep my head down or stare straight ahead. I shred inside.

I rip off my fingernails. They bleed. I see it with my own eyes. Finally I'm in charge. I know the body has power. I live it. My fingers are raw and bandaged. I use many Band-aids to cushion the tenderness. We keep them in the medicine cabinet where we have no medicine at all.

I feel like I am losing my mind and always out of breath. But I don't run. Should I collapse? I can't make a scene. Scenes are unreal and inharmonious. Once Mom collapsed getting into the car for Sunday school. My dad went over to her side of the car and lifted her into the car, off the ground. No one ever said a word about it.

I say, "I'm scared." My father says, "That's error telling you that you're scared. That's not you talking." I have many specific fears. Tests, teachers, gym class, dentists, fire drills, disagreements, shoe shopping, death, boys, birthday parties, musical chairs, and talking to grownups and kids. Add to the list: fireworks, bumble bees, kissing my grandparents, graves and coffins, and never having a boyfriend.

Each morning I wake up thinking, *What scares me today?*

Doesn't everyone? My dad reminds me, "Perfect Love casts out fear." He knows lots of memorized citations. But I don't know how to love perfectly.

At breakfast, when I see my brother, I want his life. David, the child who smiles in family pictures. My mother says, "He looks like he just stepped out of the bandbox." I'm not sure what a bandbox is, but it sounds positive to me. It sounds like it describes how my brother looks, so handsome, with blond hair, perfect body, and always smiling.

I stand behind my mother's dress when family members compliment David. I stand behind my dad when he tries to introduce me to his co-workers. I stand behind telephone poles during neighborhood games of kickball. I want to disappear. Yet from the knees up, I am not deformed. Does that count?

Each morning, my clubfeet become my everything. I pull back the covers to see if I have finally deserved my healing. When my grandma comes to see us from New Jersey, I walk into the kitchen to say hi. Minna, in her German accent, says with disgust, "Walk straight, walk straight." My mother sits next to her silently, peeling the potatoes for dinner. I always try especially hard to walk straight when Grandma visits. I try to twist each foot in the correct position, walking to the refrigerator, just to show her I can. I cannot do it for more than a few steps.

Mom never reminds Grandma that I can't help it. Every visit, "Walk straight" slides out of Grandma's mouth with such ease and cluelessness. I'm not allowed to complain about foot pain, but she calls me out on the way it looks.

Every night, in bed, woolen blankets pulled up to my chin, I ponder these big questions. My throat tightens like I might cry. I toss and turn while the sheets tangle. If I run out of fingernails, I rip off the cuticle, and then bite the skin on the tips of my fingers. I use a lot of Band-aids. My father sees my tattered fingers and says, "You don't need to do that."

Yes, I do.

School becomes hell. I don't want to stand out. I don't even want to stand up. I never raise my hand. I tell my mom I feel sick, but she tells me, "That's error." So off I go to school.

I throw up on my desk, afraid to run to the bathroom. I listen to conversations in my reading group. I have a different idea but keep my mouth shut. I'm relieved when reading group ends, and I don't get a chance to read out loud. I can take the book away from my face now.

As I get older my feet start to have thick callouses on the soles and sides, because I can only walk on tiptoe. I can't put my feet down flat. There's no even distribution of weight on my feet. Eventually, when I am around 11, I become my own podiatrist although I don't know that word yet. The pressure on my feet is intense as I walk. If I tell my dad that the bottom of my feet hurt, he reads me a hymn or tells me to turn away from the physical.

So I get a pair of sharp scissors from the kitchen drawer. I close my bedroom door and try to shave off the callouses. I've never heard of a podiatrist, not that we would go to one anyway. When I shave off the skin, sometimes the cheap scissors cut too deeply and gouge the pads of my feet.

Podiatrists cut one thin layer at a time. I dig out the whole callous at once. The area bleeds. I'm shocked when I see the blood. I dab the area with a Kleenex. We don't use Neosporin. I don't have the right instruments for a foot procedure. I patch myself up with Band-aids and put my socks and shoes back on. The bandaged areas sting. I try to walk balancing a different way. But I have to walk on the balls of my feet. The rest of the day, at home, I limp in my fluffy blue slippers.

The next day I have to wear my shoes with their leather soles. There's not much give to them. Who can I tell? Someone has to take care of my feet. So I do. My parents never look at the bottoms of my feet. They "behold the perfect man." I continue to be my own doctor.

I do what I need to do, without a word.

I wish I could tell my young self about Dr. Diresta. There are doctors who do foot procedures without drawing blood.

After surgery, at age 38, I find a local podiatrist to help me when I have an infection or some part of my foot hurts. The minute I walk in his office, full of orthopedic footwear magazines, I feel at home. The office staff calls me Peg and always makes room for me even on short notice.

Dr. Diresta comes into the cubicle, wearing a blue button-down shirt and khakis. He asks what he can do for me. The first appointment I tell him my whole story: born with clubfeet, leaving the religion, surgery, learning to walk again, still some issues. He looks at my bare feet and tells me what a talented surgeon I had. Dr. Diresta is my loyal orthopedic support. We have known each other so long now that we talk about our families and our hobbies and laugh about the sad state of politics. He never lectures me about the arthritis I have in my feet, ankles, and knees from waiting so long for surgery. Only once, as he shaved off a callous, he asked what made me wait so long. When I started to tell him my long tale, he looked like he might cry.

He said quietly, "That must have been so hard."

Dr. Diresta is a master at getting my feet so they don't hurt for another two to three weeks. I never forget to tell him how his expertise enables me to make up for lost time.

I wish I'd known as a youngster that I'd be able to tell my story someday to a caring doctor.

THE AXIS OF FAMILY LIFE

There is a lot you can't change when you are a kid. But you can pack for the journey...

Jeanette Winterson

Home, a comfort, a symbol.

Its portrait, though just a building, hung in our dining room.

No portraits of other family members hung anywhere else in the house.

By 11, I roamed freely in any part of the Mother Church. I knew what hid behind each massive door, up each marble staircase, and in each balcony. I knew the secret location where they counted Sunday's collection on Monday mornings, a secret room in the third balcony.

Each week I arrived an hour early. While my parents prepared for teaching Sunday school, I explored. I opened a mini-door half way up a flight of stairs and crept up the narrow, back stairway to the original sanctuary. Each window in this tiny church was beautifully ornate with stained glass. I fingered the thick pieces that depicted Jesus' healings.

Bible verses and Science and Health citations were inscribed in gold leaf on the walls. Those two books are our "pastors." To my left: "Ye shall know the truth, and the truth will make you free." To my right: "Divine Love always has met and, always will meet, every human need." They gave me a rush of healing anticipation.

I sat in the antique mahogany pews and gazed at the beauty. The green velvet cushions filled with stiff horsehair, were uncomfortable, kind of like my grandma's mattress.

Long ago the sermon was read from a raised platform at the front here. The tall brass lights on each side must have cast a soft, warm shadow on the congregation. The small pipe organ was tucked underneath this platform. That's where the organist for the bigger church, in this same building, practiced every Sunday morning. My dad first showed me this refuge.

Now I owned it.

Walking back downstairs, I took special care on the slippery marble stairs. The brass banisters and the mosaic tiles in the entrance to the vestry, which housed the Sunday school, had the elegance of any art museum. All the rooms in the church were under one massive dome.

Driving into the Back Bay, I recognized it in the Boston skyline. The most beautiful and authoritative of my family members, for sure.

The hymns I sang each week with my Sunday school classmates reminded me of prayers put to music. During the week I sang the hymns to myself, giving me courage to leave the house for school.

Of course, I knew the history of the religion and its founder. It was the only subject at our dinner table. Its heightened importance was logical. My dad worked for the Mother Church, the headquarters of the Christian Science Church. It was his calling and the center of our family's world. He corrected, through writing or interview, what the church considered false newspaper or tv reports about the religion.

I loved going to his office after church on Sundays, when he needed to pick up something. David and I ran down the narrow corridor to his office to see who could be first on his swivel chair. I was so proud to see his name on the door. His office smelled like leather-bound books. His pencils, newly sharpened. A picture of the religious founder hung on the empty wall to the left.

Monday through Friday, Dad lobbied to get legislation passed in the US to safeguard exemptions from vaccinations or physical exams in public schools. He lobbied to convince insurance companies of Christian Science's safety as a viable alternative to medical care. His work provided support to parents and legal protection from prison if their children died under Christian Science care. I heard him talking with his boss on the phone every time that happened.

It terrified me thinking about children dying from trusting God. Sometimes I couldn't sleep, hoping it never happened to my brother or me.

For Dad it wasn't a 9-5 job. He was working for a "cause." Church wasn't just on Sundays for any of us. It didn't matter that not many people thought our way of life made sense. We stayed on the same page as Dad. I never wanted to be called a "dissident," a church member who decided to disagree with the teachings.

Why not go to doctors, when they could so easily treat run-of-the-mill illnesses? My dad told me that Christian Science healings were instantaneous and complete. On a higher level.

I hadn't had one of those yet, but it sounded thrilling.

At school, my "blue card" exempted me from eye tests and hearing tests. Mom turned in the card to the nurse's office each September. When the nurse came into my classroom each year to line the class up for an eye exam, I'd find the guts to say, "I have a blue card. I'm a Christian Scientist." I saw all my classmates staring at me.

And was the nurse shaking her head? Bad enough to stand out physically with my clubfeet, without calling further attention on me these days. I sat in my classroom, with my stomach in knots, while the rest of the class went with the nurse and my teacher down the hall.

I didn't ask to be the ambassador for Truth.

I learned God was in control of my body although my clubfeet showed me otherwise. I didn't need any eye or ear exam. God was my healer. But I never tried explaining to my friends.

They'd never have understood. And then many years later I couldn't understand either. So, ever so gradually, I let go of that axis.

Prying my fingers off, embarrassed by my failure.

THESE ARE NOT MY PEOPLE

I sat on the narrow brick stoop. I waved goodbye to my dad as his carpool picked him up. The brown leaves swirled and made a vortex by the corner of our house by the black mailbox.

I am in the wrong family, a voice whispered. My stomach fell to my ugly brown shoes. I felt the goose bumps under my fall jacket. This unsettling voice lodged in my 8-year-old body. If I forgot that statement for a day or so, the voice reminded me with the same startling sentence.

I looked for clues. Maybe I'd been adopted and was out of synch with the real Cooks. I wasn't tall and lean. That I was cranky is an understatement, not an even-keeled pleaser, like my brother. I was the source of constant "inharmony" as my dad accused with his righteous voice. "Call me Lee," I used to say.

"I'm not Peggy." They just laughed. I was so much more than they wanted.

Convivial dinnertime conversation seemed impossible. I was not interested in small talk or listening to my dad talk about his work. I had her own questions and opinions. "What if the virgin birth is fake?" "What if a man wants to marry a man?" "I don't think Jesus really ascended."

"Oh, honey, you don't really mean that." My mom hoped I'd retract the blasphemy.

One evening after dinner, I asked my mom if I could see my birth certificate. There might be parents out there that belonged to me. The family birth certificates were locked in a red metal box under my parents' bed. Yes, these were my parents. Theodore N. Cook, writer, it stated. Charlotte M. Cook, housewife. So evidently I lived in the right family but belonged to the wrong clan.

Jean Shinoda Bolen in her book, *Crossing to Avalon*, describes strategies children use to cope like who have been abused. They either act out negatively or if lucky, they might tell themselves a story to get through childhood, a story like "These are not my people." Sometimes, she explains, if the child is fortunate, the story she tells herself comes true. She creates her own myth until she can change her reality.

Perhaps the voice that said, "You are in the wrong family," was actually meant to be a comforting voice. You are in the wrong family, but do not fear. Maybe that voice was meant to be the beginning of my own myth. At the time, I interpreted it as a fearful, haunting voice. I was sure I didn't belong anywhere or to anyone. But the voice could have meant, "You do not belong here, but you will find your way."

There was no physical abuse. It was certainly not life and death to find my people immediately. However, a yellow behavior chart pinned on the kitchen wall with my name in bold black marker verified my negative standing. "Peggy is loving, Peggy listens to God, Peggy is pleasant at dinner." No stars on that chart.

My fierce emotions scared me and my family even worse. "Why are *my* feet crooked?" "Why doesn't God *ever* help me?"

"This is not you talking. This is just error." My parents used that, "not you talking" line to make me feel insane, I was sure.

"It's not error, it's me," I snarled.

By upper elementary school I began to dive into nature, books, art and loud music. I created my own private reality when not lying face down on my bedspread in a funk. When my family went on one-week summer vacations to Maine, the shells and rocks of the coastline became my beautiful clan. My dad was always sick on vacations. My mom stayed inside bringing him toast and warm ginger ale. My brother lay on his bed reading mysteries.

I ran outside each morning. I leaped unsteadily from rock to rock with my metal pail and red slippers on, collecting shells. The ferocious white caps crashed against the rocks. Digging up smooth rocks and periwinkle shells kept me busy till noon. I laid them on my dresser in the pine-paneled cottage. I tasted the salt on my hands. I drew my ocean treasures with my new vacation crayons and pad of paper.

Later characters in books became my surrogate family. Their stories kept me company and revealed a realistic slice of life. When a character died, like Old Yeller, I was grief-stricken. I was jealous of happy families like the one in *The Little House on the Prairie* family. Sex-filled lives fascinated me, like the couple in *A Tree Grows in Brooklyn*. The first time I met anyone with clubfeet was when I read *Of Human Bondage*. The title made me cry. I kept these kindred spirits lined up on my bookshelves.

Spending a summer at Camp Newfound in Maine when I was 12, I finally met my "people."

Mattie, the "mascot" of our cabin, had a Long Island accent that pierced the night with raucous laughter. The college-aged counselors were outgoing and had a tantalizing hint of rebelliousness about them. I watched them carefully for insights on how to be cool yet personable. They were outgoing and nurturing to "their" girls. Meg and Alice were not afraid to smile and cajole the preteens out of our surly moods. The counselors laughed off small offenses, like a messy trunk or a semi-thoughtless retort. We could all be who we were or wanted to be for the summer.

Meg read Edgar Allen Poe poems after taps and scared the hell out of us with her dramatic voices and sound effects. Alice read *King Arthur and the Knights of the Round Table* out loud. They brought back forbidden treats on their nights off. We gleefully gobbled up Oreos and red licorice. In the dark, late at night, on the cabin floor, in beautiful Maine.

My cabinmates laughed at my humor and sarcastic monologues. I'd never had an audience like that before. No one told me I was being negative or not listening to God. It felt good to laugh every single day. I called home and asked to stay an extra four weeks.

We sang a hymn each morning at this religious girls' camp. The hymns made me happy here. Maybe it was singing while gazing out the window at Long Lake that gave me peace. Maybe it was the Sunday school teachers who were so young and not steeped in dogma. Sitting on the beach talking about God on Sunday mornings seemed less stressful than in Boston inside the church. God's beauty was surrounding me beneath the birches and the pines. There was no doubt here.

Often riotous laughter erupted from their cabin past taps. The assistant director gave a harsh warning with her flashlight through the screen door. "That is just about enough, Twin Pines," Pat boomed. We then cracked up again. We couldn't help it.

I canoed in the war canoe across the lake to Harrison. All 12 of us went on a donut run and then canoed back, just for fun. On the way over and back, we sang, "Our paddles clean and bright flashing like silver, dip, dip, and swing," in a round. Our voices echoed across the lake.

I swam the best I could with my weak legs. No one said a word about my feet, but I was still self-conscious. I dragged a beach towel in front of me when I wore my bathing suit to the waterfront. I wore flip-flops even though they didn't stay on very well. The rocks would have hurt my bare, sensitive feet. I passed the "big float test" so I could swim in the deep end.

The teenage campers, who lived up on the "hill," taught my cabin mates how to shave our legs on "hair wash" rock. Hair wash rock fit about five girls sitting on it in the middle of the boating side of the lake. We didn't have indoor showers at camp in 1962. I went in the cold lake with my bathing suit on and a tube of Prell in one hand. I watched the shavers wistfully from a distance. I put a dab of green Prell on my blond hair and then submerged under the water and scrubbed. When it sounded squeaky, it was clean.

I felt like a mermaid coming up for air.

The cool teenagers took my confident cabin mates one at a time up on the rock and gave shaving lessons until the lunch bell rang. I wasn't sure I was ready for this rite of passage. My mom would never approve. Mom didn't shave her own legs. But it looked like fun having private instructions on the rock.

In a few weeks I dared. I borrowed a razor from June, who had brought everything to camp, including Ban de Soleil suntan lotion and madras shorts for dances. I carefully climbed up on the rock, wearing my flip-flops for traction. When I was almost to the top of the rock, someone held out a hand to help me on the final ascent.

I sat on the sun drenched rock and watched as Kay lathered her legs with a bar of soap, held the razor, and demonstrated shaving her own legs. "Watch me carefully," she said as she switched to the other leg. Then Kay watched as her student lathered up and took the double-edged razor and shaved. Off came my thick blond leg hair. Short stroke after short stroke. No blood. I rinsed my legs with a pail of water up on the rock. Smooth as silk. I was part of the clan. I went to lunch that day feeling much older and smoother.

The "new camper report" mailed home from Meg and Alice said, "Peggy has adjusted like she has always been here and usually has us in stitches." I found the report, under some magazines, on the coffee table when I got home in mid-August.

Now I had a camp family. My people. I propped my cabin picture up on my dresser. I kept that report in my top dresser drawer under my rolled up socks. I reread my counselors' affirmations during the school year, and refolded it. Now I had a time each year when I belonged somewhere.

For so long I considered music, art, and books poor substitutes for human allies or muses. Now I realize that they were filling a void in a healthy way for me. I was sustained with quality, non-judgmental companions. My first safe allies. Then ever so timidly I made connections with peers. It always felt awkward, and like hard work, even at camp. But camp became my beautiful safe space to try out belonging.

In the winter I wrote to my cabin mates and ecstatically opened their replies. I kept these "family" letters on my desk. Right before camp started, I'd get anxious and nauseous, but I'd reread the letters from my camp friends, reminding me that I had a camp family waiting for me.

Crossing the Piscataqua River Bridge into Maine, I'd change into my sailor blue uniform in the car.

Like Jean Shinoda Bolen said, some people are lucky enough to change their story if they can just get through childhood. That sinking feeling of being in the wrong family sent me on a quest. Although it lasted longer than I wanted, I've been lucky enough to find my people and feel more at home in this world.

SHOES I HAVE KNOWN

Clubfeet put a real crimp in my shoe collection. Maybe that's why I had a shoe obsession. I imagined my life of confidence, comfort, and sex appeal if only I could wear the shoes of my dreams. I'd accessorize each dress perfectly with stylish, colorful shoes.

Growing up, I eyed a person's shoes before I noticed the person wearing them. Were they wearing loafers? How about deck shoes or clogs? I loved men's wing tips with the designs on the toe area. My mom wore open-toed heels. My friends sported shiny black "Mary Jane" patent leather shoes for birthday parties. At Easter the white satin shoes with one strap looked so springy. I would have loved to wear them to Sunday school. So natural to notice everyone's Easter shoes since I always looked down, afraid to make eye contact.

I had no choices in shoe stores as a young child. My shoes were always brown, high top, tie shoes with a wedge on the outer edge to keep my feet from rolling over. The local cobbler carved the wedges out of leather and glued them on after we bought the orthopedic shoes. The leather soles and wedges made my shoes slippery. I had to be careful not to fall on the polished linoleum floors at school.

In the 1950s, I wore dresses or skirts to school, so it was impossible to hide my hideous shoes. I wanted to be a boy so my pants covered my eyesores, as far to the ground as possible. Boys wore tie shoes or high top sneakers and didn't worry about fashion. I flinched when I received the class picture each year. I stood out in the front row with those awful crooked feet and misshapen shoes. I had also inherited the short genes. I'd always hide in the back row until the class photographer pulled me up front, right in the middle of the picture. I'd grimace and squint until the ordeal ended.

My father polished my shoes in the cellar each night with brown Kiwi polish. I think it was his way of apologizing for my angst or maybe his own. He knew deep down how unattractive my shoes were, even though my parents kept the "party line." "These shoes have such good support," they said.

I wore the high top brown shoes for years until the orthopedic shoe man made a fatal verbal faux pas. The owner of the shoe store, Mr. Maripotti, wanted to be a foot doctor as a young man. He knew everything about foot deformities. He didn't have the funds for medical school in the 1940s. He told me his story once, while lacing up my new shoes.

That's why he opened a specialty shoe store for people like me.

One Saturday in the fall, he reported to my mother that I really needed surgery soon to correct my feet. He mentioned, "They're getting worse."

I sat stunned. The truth was so scary. And I so rarely heard it.

Mom and Dad didn't know that the last time I sat at this store, I'd glanced down on the index card with my name on it. Mr. Maripotti had left the card on the bench while he looked for my size. I saw the word "clubfeet." We had always called my feet, "the problem" and that I walked "crooked."

I had to look up the definition and diagnosis of this stunning name: clubfeet, at home, in the encyclopedia. But now during this visit, he'd verbalized his opinion about surgery, while leaning down tying my new shoes. Mom quickly paid for the shoes and we rushed to the car.

I cried all the way home in the front seat. "I'm not going there again ever," I wailed, feeling my lunch rising into my throat. My mom paid attention to the signs for Needham and didn't say much.

What if he kept badgering us? The thought terrified me. My mom wouldn't share our religious beliefs with Mr. Maripotti. There'd be no explanation or confrontation especially where other customers could overhear. It just wasn't Mom's soft spoken way. I'm sure for Mr. Maripotti watching a school-age customer never getting medical treatment seemed odd, perhaps even negligent.

I knew there'd be no surgery. I couldn't imagine ever going under ether again. I couldn't imagine missing weeks of school. I'd be so far behind. And I'd come back with casts or crutches. I'd die of embarrassment. Surgery was only offered as a threat at my house anyway. "If you can't be receptive to God, maybe we should just go to the hospital."

Always the fear of a surprise surgery somewhere in the back of my fretful mind.

When we arrived home, I stormed in the front door, my face soaking wet and my heart shocked and enraged. My father opened his office door and yelled, "What's going on?" I screamed at him that I hated my new shoes and hated Mr. Maripotti. Maybe he'd come downstairs and talk to me.

I slammed the door to my bedroom and sat alone on the edge of my bed until dinnertime.

My heart crashed through my chest. I listened for footsteps as I wept. Nothing.

Solitude.

From then on I went to Stephen's Shoe Store in our town. Mr. Weinstein, the owner, obviously saw I had a severe foot "problem" but never asked questions. He searched the back room for a pair that fit me. Who can find EEEE shoes in a regular shoe store? He spent several minutes behind the brown curtain rummaging around and appeared with two boxes. His smile gave me hope. I loved him from the first meeting.

He found one pair, grey suede Hush Puppies. Not the shoes of my dreams and the back rubbed against the place where my heel should be. I knew they'd give me blisters. I hated to tell him they didn't feel right, after all his effort. But it didn't bother him one bit. So we tried the last pair. Cobalt blue, with scalloped sides in soft suede, black laces with a raised heel. Kind of ugly but artsy in a way. No one else at school would be sporting a pair like this. So grateful to have a pair not rubbing my heels raw.

I always wondered where these odd pairs of shoes came from. Maybe they were samples from the manufacturer. I left knowing I had an ally in Mr. Weinstein. I'd just met him, and there he was searching for a pair of shoes that didn't humiliate, a person who lived compassion.

When I passed his store window on weekends, he waved, sometimes even coming to the door to say hi. I had no fear of looking him in the eye and waving back. To have an ally like him, in the center of my town, where I'd been slinking around like an untouchable, felt like an immense gift. He wasn't a church person who *had* to be kind to me. He chose me, clubfeet and all, to foster a friendship.

Shoe shopping with my mom was daunting enough. But in my early years when we shoe-shopped for the rest of the family, I just couldn't get in the mood. We drove our Rambler on a Friday night to The Barn, a shoe outlet in a neighboring city.

Mom, Dad and David talked about what kind of shoes they needed on the drive. We descended a steep hill and parked in the gravel parking lot. We crossed the street together to the one-story flat-roofed warehouse. There were thousands of shoes in there. The leather smell enveloped me. My stomach always ached in this store.

I knew there'd never be any shoes here for me. Girls who shopped here had normal width and normal shaped feet. They didn't need extra "support." Everyone who came here, I was sure, had heels.

My brother wandered around with my mom looking for his shoes. My brother's feet, long, straight, and perfect, so easy to fit. If I had been born first, would my feet look like his?

David needed to find white bucks for marching in the band. The soles of bucks were smooth red rubber, comfortable for marching on the field or in town parades. What would happen to me when I got to junior high and needed bucks for the Memorial Day parade? Would I stop playing my clarinet and quit the band? I always worried way ahead of time. I imagined the worst, the most embarrassing scenarios.

Next David looked for sneakers for gym, a pair of high-top black Keds. I loved Keds with their blue rectangle on the back. I longed for red Keds. But low top sneakers came right off my feet. No high-top Reeboks for girls in the 50s. I bit my lip.

I wandered away and looked at shoelaces. They had every length and color by the cash register. Socks, though, were my consolation prize.

The Barn had a small sock section by the door. Wigwams. I loved the name. I ran my hands along the section and felt the fabrics. I chose a pair of blue knee socks. Knee socks made me feel less conspicuous. When I covered my legs, I felt, in a strange way, like my feet were disguised too. Tights covered even better, but it was still fall this Friday night. No tights until December.

When I found my mom, she sat in the women's department trying on open-toed, high-heeled shoes for church. She took forever to make a decision. She had slender feet, size 8AA. I'd never be able to wear high heels. What will I wear when I'm a woman? I didn't dare ask.

The man at the register gave the shoe buyers big bags with a red barn on them, cinched shut with white chord. He asked if I needed a bag for my socks?

"I'll just carry them in my hands," I answered.

Luckily, Friday nights at the Barn happened only two times a year. I felt ragged and nasty on the way home. Jealous and full of despair. Doomed to never fit in.

I held in my wrath through two towns and one highway. About three streets from home, I had to say something obnoxious or use a rude tone. My dad called it "grousing" and sharply demanded I stop. He knew, from experience, that the more I "groused," the more emotional the ride up our street became. Sometimes I had the conscious urge to draw everyone into my misery, just so they knew how I felt. But Dad was never in the mood for long drawn-out crying scenes. I always ended up asking why God refused to heal me.

Dad preached that I needed to be more "receptive to Truth."

SATURDAY AT THE DUMP

My memory knows more about me than I do. It doesn't lose what deserves to be saved.

Eduardo Galeano

Dad and I dragged the dented trashcans out from the garage and unlocked the trunk of the car. We hoisted the cans into the trunk. Dad tied the hood loop around the massive bumper of the Ford Falcon with a laundry line. The trashcans secured, it didn't matter if we stopped short or took a sharp corner. Then off to the Needham Disposal Area, better known as the town dump, our ritual each Saturday from my early childhood to probably age 12.

Unneeded paper crackled and burned in the back yard on Friday nights. The flames jumped high in the steel incinerator, always missing the maple trees off to the left. Saturday, everything but paper came with us. Dog food tins, black banana peels, rinds of grapefruits and oranges, moldy bread, and gooey eggshells filled the cans.

I sat in the middle of the front seat next to Dad. No seat belts or bucket seats in those days, just a long bench. I waved to our neighbors, the Kimuras, as we headed out.

My Saturday adventure. Just he and I.

I really wanted to be useful to my dad, so he'd need me around. I didn't have the pushing power to mow the lawn with our hand mower, like David. And in winter, Dad and David heaved soaking snow to the driveway borders. But Dad proclaimed me "good company" on these Saturday morning runs. High praise for someone a bit stingy with compliments. And I wanted to pitch in and appear capable to Dad.

Even though I often imagined myself a lowly slug, schlepping along in my orthopedic shoes.

Going with Dad alone made me feel special but sometimes anxious. Dad always maintained self-control. Me, I cried or lashed out dramatically at perceived inequalities in our family constellation or in the world. I longed to measure up in Dad's eyes. I never knew how to do that. I ended up always asking him lots of questions to fill the quiet on these Saturday errands.

Did his dad teach him to drive a stick shift? When did he know he could draw so well? How did he become so ill in World War II? If I ran out of things to ask, I listened to the car radio or kicked my dangling legs up and down.

My writing about "Saturday at the Dump" seemed a simple story of a tradition Dad and I had each Saturday in my early years. However as I started writing the story, instead of reminiscing fondly about our mornings together, I began to feel uneasy.

Perhaps as a child I remembered being driven to the hospital for casts as a baby/young child against my will. Unsafe surprises kept me off balance. Maybe after all these years I was still being triggered.

Was this really just a "dump run?" Did the memory of mom and dad taking me for my smallpox inoculation for Kindergarten rise up? There were no religious exemptions for smallpox vaccines. Mom and Dad told me, "We're going for a little ride. Hop in." And then later, "We'll stop here to get you a drink of water." But not a drink in sight, but a doctor's office.

At least it was just Dad and I on those Saturday mornings. I had his full attention. In the afternoon he'd enclose himself in his study doing office work. As a church official, he might be typing a rough draft of a letter to a dissident member of the church or a script for the radio show the church produced. Sometimes I could hear him through the door in hushed tones, speaking church jargon to his boss. Sometimes Dad told David and me to "quiet down" if we forgot and practiced our musical instruments during his official phone calls.

Mom spent Saturday afternoons at American Beauty getting her hair done.

Besides writing for our church, Dad was an artist and I wanted to be one too. He could draw an armadillo freehand and make it look real.

Once, when he stayed home from work, sick with a cold, he took an old Whitman's chocolate sampler box and made me a cardboard mini dollhouse. He crafted rooms with cardboard dividers and colored paper wallpaper, just like the floor plan of our house. He even cut out a brown cardboard mini-tv with a cowboy drawn on the screen.

I think I favored an abstract style because I couldn't compete with his realistic masterpieces.

The bookcases in his study brimmed with hardbound art books. I loved comparing Van Gogh to Renoir to Monet. I sat on the floor on rainy weekdays after school and turned the glossy pages in the oversized books swirling with vivid colors.

In the corner of the study he kept an old wooden art box he'd used in college. Opening the clasp, I was hit by the smell of oil paints and turpentine wafting out. The tubes, somewhat dried up and cracked, had mysterious names like Prussian Blue, Venetian Red, and Cadmium Yellow. His paintbrushes, meticulously cleaned, became mine when I started art classes in first grade.

That room became my own private sanctuary while Dad worked in Boston.

We might have been kindred spirits back then, but when I wanted him to encourage me to follow an artist's path, he didn't although it was fine to double major in Education and Studio Art.

"You are so good with kids," my mom always said. "Always something to fall back on, if you teach." For a long time, I couldn't figure out what I was supposed to be doing before the great "fall back."

Disenchanted, I realized even Dad thought art was a hobby or an activity to do on a rainy day although he had been a studio art major in college.

During my senior year in college, I told him I wanted to be a silk-screen artist. I relished spending time in the college's ultra-modern art studio infused with paint fumes, creating posters, wall hangings, and textile designs.

"That's nice, honey."

Such a disappointing response from my no-longer kindred spirit.

Art is an unreliable income, at best, but I took it so personally, like he thought I wasn't talented enough (which I probably wasn't, but let me figure it out). Perhaps that was his way of loving, of keeping me from added disappointment. I was not strong enough to pursue art professionally without his blessing, yet he remained my intellectual hero and my artist in residence.

On those Saturdays so long ago, Dad had a prescribed schedule to keep. While on weekdays he got up at five am sharp to pray, he was out of bed by seven on Saturdays. At daylight he turned on WCRB, very calming and classical. Dad wore his weekend chinos, his blue sneakers, and short-sleeved button-down plaid shirt. He always wore the same old green parka if it was winter. His graying hair was always in place parted on the side. Every summer he spiced up his life at the barber shop with a "whiffle." Even on Saturdays he smelled like Mennen Aftershave.

Sometimes he wore a baseball cap. Not a cool one from the Red Sox, but one with netting for ventilation and a brim for keeping the sun from shining on the lenses of his glasses. The lenses were so thick that when I tried them on, I couldn't see a thing and felt dizzy.

He wore Mom's gold high school ring on his right pinkie. He told me it was kind of like his engagement ring from my mom. A gold watch, a wedding ring, and Mom's high school ring were all his trinkets. His prized, gold Phi Beta Kappa key from Columbia he kept boxed to the left in his top bureau drawer.

On our way to the dump, we drove slowly through the neighborhoods and arrived in the center of town. No town would have a dump smack dab in the center so we continued on past the stores and stopped for gas.

In the 50s it was cash only, so Dad told Vic at Donnatti's, "Two dollars' worth of the regular, please." Vic checked the oil and cleaned the windshield, using his squeegee to make clean lines.

We were on a first-name basis with Vic. Our second-hand cars always needed some new brake rotors or engine work. We spent a lot of time walking to Vic's, retrieving our repaired cars.

Dad's hands didn't look like they should be hauling garbage cans to a dump. He had slender fingers and smooth artist's hands. Perfect fingernails, not like mine bitten to the quick. Grandma Cook and I had the same bad habit. Dad never seemed to have dirty fingernails or hands, even when he painted the house or planted zinnias. He never smelled sweaty either.

I look back now on his clean hands as a metaphor for how he lived his life. Following the religion kept his hands clean from all those medical decisions that life would have required. It was safe to work for the church. It was what he knew best.

As a ghostwriter for the church, he never had to sign his own name on unpleasant edicts he wrote for the Board of Directors. No trail of dirt left behind.

We rattled on to the other end of town, the end with new construction on streets newly named Country Way, Winding River Road, and Charles River Drive. My dad called these new homes "swanky." Not like the section we lived in, "Birds Hill," with its modest Cape Cod architecture and split-levels. Even one garage, a luxury.

I knew we were getting close to our first destination because sea gulls swooped over the area, flapping and screaming. Dad told me sea gulls loved the leftover food scraps in the dump, even with the bulldozers riding over the heaps. The gulls swooped in and out, flying away with breakfast. We never quite knew what we'd see poking out of a rancid mound as we drove in: an old chair, a sink, a tennis racket twirling through the air.

We headed to the biggest, ripest mound, and the man directed Dad to stop the car. Dad untied the trunk. It was too stinky for me, and wearing my school shoes, I stayed put.

The unending heaps of discards headed towards the horizon. Two yellow bulldozers rode up and down the trashy mounds. They pushed and flattened the heaps, struggling to stay upright.

I imagined picking over those interesting mounds for collage materials. Instead I looked out the rearview mirror and saw the line of cars behind us ready to take our place. Sometimes I'd see a doll's head or a pizza box go flipping away in the wind as the great mix churned. That head flipping around in the wind was the whirlwind that lived within me, feeling often that I might just flip out and lose my mind.

When he was done, my dad knocked the dirt off his sneaker treads on the side of the tire and got back in. The worker tied the empty cans back in the trunk. Trash cans clattering, we negotiated the potholes to the exit.

Luckily, Dad never smelled like the dump for too long. We'd open the car windows after the drop-off, and soon his Mennen essence took over again.

The next week we'd go back again, but this time the heaps were over to the left or then to the right. Sometimes the heaps were even paved over. The path to the dump kept getting further and further away from the entrance as the years went on.

Just like my path to spiritual healing.

Dad and I never stopped for a snack or treat. We just headed home and dragged the trashcans back into the garage.

If I could have slipped in next to the young girl in the car, I'd have whispered in her ear:

You are not crazy. What you are feeling is real. I'm going to find a good clubfoot doctor. I'm going to show you that people solve problems in more than one way. I know you so well, you'd have screamed, "NO, I can't show my feet to anyone." But I would have tenderly said, *It's okay to be scared. I'll be with you each step of the way. You're not alone anymore. We can do this. I can help you be brave.*

THE MASTER OF ELMER'S GLUE

My aunt's slanted left-handwriting, a giveaway on the brown outer package. Aunt Gloria mailed a delicate porcelain set of tiny cups and saucers and plates for tea parties with my dolls. A perfect birthday present. The Chinese blue and white willow pattern, had little birds flying above. I'd never seen a pattern like that. I couldn't stop imagining this delicate gift all day at school.

The instant I got home, I took the pieces out of their protective covering and set up shop. I put my quilted doll blanket on my bedroom floor. I set the picnic for one stuffed bunny and two dolls, whose legs bent easily so they could sit on the floor with me. The quilted square blanket, a bit tattered, morphed into elegance with the place settings at each corner.

Aunt Gloria, childless, had a sixth sense when gift giving. Whether it was the pink radio, the fancy blue dress with NO smocking, or the gumball machine, she never disappointed. Her unique greeting cards were just as distinctive with slots filled with shiny silver dimes.

After my birthday dinner and phone calls from my grandparents, I bathed and got ready for bed. By now my tea set sat on a table in the living room. I had taken it upstairs to display with my birthday cards and new knee socks from my parents and the china miniature horse from David. I had a doll suitcase with a brass latch that could hold this magnificent gift. It was tan, with a red plastic handle. I started to pack it all up. I tenderly wrapped each cup, saucer, plate, and teapot in the tissue paper that came with my new dress and the delicate horse.

Birthdays usually scared me as all the attention was on me. I detested being sung to and several childhood birthday pictures show me with my fingers in my ears, trying to avoid the song, if not the camera's flash. But this had been a happy birthday. My favorite dinner of pork chops and applesauce. The chocolate cake with magical marshmallow frosting and huge gumdrops around the edges. Pink candles and the revolving cake plate. Just my family watching.

The principal of our school had been absent that day, so I didn't have to walk up the stairs to the stage while he played happy birthday on the piano, the whole cafeteria staring. I dreaded this each year. Mr. Jenkins was so thoughtful to do this for each child at Broadmeadow School. I loved it when we sang to the kids unless it was *my* birthday.

All bathed, I said goodnight and picked up the suitcase packed with my china.

I headed to the staircase in our split-level house, and as I went down the first step, the latch on the suitcase sprang open, and all my brand new china tumbled down the uncarpeted stairs.

I heard the cracks and the bangs in slow motion, as the shattered pieces, still wrapped in tissue, clattered to the bottom.

The suitcase lid was wide open and I gave out a wail.

I sat in the hallway, on the linoleum floor feeling each wad of tissue and the myriad pieces underneath. Mom and Dad heard the smashing china and came to the bottom of the steps where I sat in a heap. I cried and cried, both for my stupidity at putting them in this rather old doll suitcase and for the perfect birthday present now in pieces.

Both my parents had tender hearts. Mom got me settled in bed, my pillowcase wet with tears. Dad hugged me good night and said he thought he could repair my precious cups and saucers. He was the master of Elmer's Glue.

When I came upstairs for breakfast the next morning, there on the kitchen table was the cobbled together tea set sitting on newspaper drying. Some pieces had six or seven seams. Some chips were missing, but the shapes nevertheless were cobbled together. Each piece stood on its own again. Dad had stayed up past midnight gluing and then reinforcing with bits of tissue on the insides of each shattered piece.

Dad at his most tender. At his most giving. At his most artistic, meticulous self.

Wrapping my arms around him, my cheek against his brown tweed sports jacket, Dad explained the repairing process to me. My tea set was never the same, of course, as glue lines browned with age. But it remained my precious gift.

Unpacking a box as we weeded out the house after Mom died, I found the set wrapped in newspaper. The joy and sorrow of that birthday surged back. And then I remembered the night-long repair.

A living homage to my father's love.

UNDER THE RACK

Within silence our own voice dwells.

Terry Tempest Williams

The only store I liked more than Woolworth's, for its hotdogs and orange sodas, had to be W. T. Grant's. A pet section lined the back wall. Every Saturday I asked my mom to come and gaze at the cages with me. After her grocery shopping was finished next door, she came with me to see the creatures I liked best.

There were always some baby turtles, goldfish, or turquoise and yellow parakeets that I secretly wished I could buy. I had no money, so I observed and fantasized.

One Saturday, after gazing into the creatures' cages, my mom and I ran into a classmate's mother, Mrs. James, near the entrance. The minute I saw her I recognized whose mom she was. My stomach began to churn. Her daughter, Jeanne, had cerebral palsy. There was something about seeing Jeanne's mom that made my clubfeet seem more real. That mom knew what she saw. She was not in a God-induced coma.

Mrs. James cornered my mom and began to comment on how sad it was both of these "beautiful" girls had birth defects. She started telling my mom the date when Joan was having her next surgery to loosen her tight heel chords. She wondered when I'd be getting surgery to straighten my feet?

My ears started ringing and I gulped in air. I slid under a circular girls clothing rack nearby. The tags on each piece of clothing were white and dangled like Christmas lights. I sat down on the floor, camouflaged, I hoped.

Neither mother told me to stand up, and what was I thinking? They must have seen me.

I tried to listen, yet I didn't want to. My mom was saying, "Uh huh, uh huh." Not adding anything to the conversation, since it was not conducive to "healing." In our religion, we didn't discuss birth defects. That was totally inappropriate for one expecting a miracle from God.

When would Jeanne's mom leave? When would she stop talking? Would a saleslady see me and pull me up off the floor? I moved closer to the center under the rack and looked up at the colorful jumpers. I smelled that starched fabric smell.

So, there was my mom on ground level in total avoidance mode, and I was in avoidance under the rack. Like mother, like daughter.

Poor Mrs. James must have been so disappointed not to get some empathy or kindred spirit discussion. My mom certainly could understand her grief.

Avoidance had a certain look. And Jeanne and I had the façade down. We both kept those steely, don't look at me, glares, as we walked the school halls. Only Jeanne's mom could handle reality.

DYING OF STARVATION

I am dying of starvation.

There is no food that fills me.

The kitchen shelves are stocked.

On Saturday mornings sneaking into the kitchen at dawn, I slowly open the utensil drawer to ease out a knife. On top of the refrigerator my mom hides the angel food cake. It is a special treat from Stop and Shop. I prefer a denser cake for true gorging, but the strawberry icing makes up for the fluff of the cake. I cut a piece just big enough not to be noticed. I put the whole piece in my mouth at once and lick my fingers.

I don't run the kitchen faucet this early. I wipe off the knife with a napkin. I need more. I am an 8-year-old cake thief.

I wait until breakfast for the donut run. My father drives to the local donut store with the clown logo. Donuts should make me happy. I ride with him imagining the thick lemon cream in my mouth. Two jellies, two lemon, two chocolate, two coconut. The smell of dough kisses me as I push in the heavy door. I open the waxed bag as I walk back to the car and take another whiff.

Drive fast, I think. In our family we don't take a bite until we are all sitting down together.

Two donuts apiece. Even if I only have room for one, I eat both. Cake and donuts and orange juice swish in my stomach all morning. The sweet turns to sour as I make a bathroom run.

I warm up Clams à la King and Minute Rice Friday after school in junior high. The creamy globs of chunky clam soup mixed with the rice creates a heavy glue. I don't stop eating until I feel quite sick enough.

On Thanksgiving I want to eat the entire bowl of stuffing. The herbs and butter and celery/parsley mix take over the house. Roasted in the turkey, it's an irresistible smell. I should be grateful.

I want to cry as my family gathers around the table. I am alone. I have nothing to say. I have so much to say. "Please pass the gravy." I smother the stuffing with the rich brown rue my mother expertly creates. Not one lump.

The morning after Thanksgiving I glide into the kitchen in my fluffy slippers and open the refrigerator. I lift the plate off the brown bowl and take a hunk of stuffing with my hands. I love the smell on my hands. The butter in it makes my hands greasy. Just one lump, so no one can tell.

I pilfer this popular leftover. I have to. The stuffing level goes down.

When my mom goes to form the leftovers into little balls to warm up in the gravy she comments, "I thought we had more stuffing than this." I quickly open the utensil drawer and noisily take out forks, knives, and spoons. Like a good girl I set the table.

I know I have gotten my share. I need more than my share. I need it to keep from starving. No one says, "Here, you deserve more." Or "This will make up for how you feel."

I am short, 5'1" and cannot afford to eat too many cookies or donuts without moving into a size 12. In those days that size is big enough for someone my age. My brother calls me "Thunder Thighs."

My brother, 6'3" by 13, pigs out on multiple bologna sandwiches after school at the kitchen table, without anyone raising an eyebrow. I eat extra slabs of bologna in front of the opened refrigerator and quickly rewrap the deli paper.

On the way home from trips to New Jersey, the cookie tin is packed with Minna's homemade tollhouse cookies under the passenger seat where I am sitting. We have assigned seats. David is behind my dad. Second in power. I am behind my mom, no power. But I can reach the cookies. I wait until dark and reach down under the seat and silently guide the tin lid off the top.

Why bother asking permission? They'd have told me I wasn't hungry. I take one cookie and stuff it in my mouth. The dough mixed with the walnuts and chocolate is so soothing.

Can't they smell it?

I swallow it in a bite or two. I take two more. The roof of my mouth hurts with the double whammy of two sweet cookies at once. The chocolate chips grate on my palate, but I don't stop yet. After four cookies, I lean over and try to rearrange them so the volume looks the same.

I let someone else carry them in the house. I have not touched them.

When I am old enough, I ride my bike alone to Needham center each Saturday. I sit at the Woolworth's counter and wait for my grilled hot dog in a roll and orange soda. I like the 99-cent price. I could eat three.

Next door is Brigham's. I order a two-scoop mocha almond cone with sprinkles. I sit alone in a booth and let the coolness soothe. The table feels a little sticky and smells like ice cream. I watch the workers hand-pack gallons, quarts, and pints of my favorite food group.

I covet their jobs: companionship with ice cream, hot fudge, marshmallow, and salted pecans. The candy counter is to the right. I watch the young teenager in her uniform cut the fudge and penuche into squares. I want to work here someday.

I cross the street quickly. There is a bathroom at the Crest, a newspaper store.

Enough is often too much.

THE MONSTROSITY

My father named the oversized dresser "the monstrosity." The monstrosity was a mahogany highboy dresser. An inheritance given to my mother by her beloved Tanta Anna, who helped my grandfather raise my mother, Dottie. My mom's birth mother died a few days after giving birth to Mom.

My grandfather remarried two years later, but Tanta Anna didn't go back to Germany. She moved from New Jersey to upstate New York and remained Mom's confidante. She called my mother "my dear child." She introduced my mom to a radical religion, Christian Science.

What makes Dad call that special inheritance a monstrosity? Only later, I realize where my sarcasm originates.

The monstrosity looms in a corner of my bedroom. Because my dad thinks it's ugly, I do too. "Can't it stand in the hallway or dining room," I nag. I beg to have it taken out of my room. But it's too big for our miniscule dining room. "Why can't David have it in his room?" "Why can't it go into the basement?" I am mouthy.

My mom cries when we complain about the monstrosity as if it's a person. She is not good at defending her opinions. She usually cries during disagreements. She cries like a child, not able to use her words to visualize her equal footing in the marriage. And then of course, my dad wins. She has an inferiority complex. He has a superiority complex. Not a great match for marital harmony.

Why didn't she tell us all to knock it off? Can't she explain why a gift given by a deceased, loved relative is something of value? Not if you've never had a voice in decision-making. There's too much emotion connected with this piece and not enough respect for Mom's feelings.

Maybe it also had something to do with our religious teachings that death is unreal. To grieve means we don't understand God's allness. We don't need something physical to remember our loved ones. But Mom did. Dogma did not hold a candle to emotion in her life.

Being so nosey, it's not surprising that I decide to explore all the drawers in this wooden beast. Mom is out doing errands; Dad is upstairs in his study. I drag a kitchen chair downstairs to my bedroom to reach the top two drawers. I am sure there must be amazing treasures stored in them. I start with the bottom two. There's one on each side over its curvy legs.

When I tug the one on the left, the metal handle rattles like it might fall off. It is full of musty-smelling old mittens and gloves. Some of the adult gloves are cracked leather with grey tattered linings. They are water-stained and stiff. Our pilled knitted red and blue mittens are too small for David and I now, but they are jammed in that drawer, too. Handmade by my Aunt Gloria, Dad's sister.

The small drawer to the right holds old valentine, anniversary, and birthday cards. Our scrawly little handwriting and hearts decorate them. They are in no particular order of holiday or year. I have to tug that jammed, overstuffed drawer to open it. I have no idea if the contents of these two bottom drawers give particular clues about Mom.

I already know she is a packrat. That's what my father calls her. These drawers are probably full of random junk, just like the linen closets and coat closets in our house.

I open the first long drawer. It holds new tablecloths and matching napkins. Some are still wrapped in white tissue paper and in their original boxes. The folds and creases are perfect. There are no gift cards in the box. Maybe they are wedding gifts. Maybe they belong to Tanta Anna. They have never been used. Maybe they are too special to risk staining.

Our family does not do formal entertaining anyway. My mom wants to invite church people over for dinner Saturday nights, but Dad says she doesn't know how to set a formal table correctly. Mom stops asking Dad about inviting company on weekends.

The next drawer is layered with old baby clothes, each wrapped in yellowing tissue. A tiny blue smocked dress from my aunt is folded neatly. The smocking is beautiful in pink and white. There are several mini baby undershirts made by Carter's. A pale blue coat lined in satin

and little baby hat with a white bow lies in a crushed box. I find one
toddler's red shoe, a Mary Jane, in the corner of that drawer.

There's a pale green knitted romper with moth holes. It must be
David's. Mom would never put me in green. In one Filene's box, there
is a mound of fluff. It looks like a mouse got in the drawer. When I
pull it out, fur flies up my nose. I see it is a girl's muff with two tiny fur
mittens. They're disintegrating. I remember seeing pictures of me with
my hands in that muff in the winter in front of the Mother Church.
These artifacts are safe from any donating marauders in the family.

The top drawer is not as deep as the others. It has a keyhole in the
middle of it, but it's not locked. I can't imagine what fits in such a
narrow drawer. Still on the chair, I pull the drawer closer to me.
Something's rattling. Sterling silver candlesticks wrapped in grey felt
bags and tarnished silverware fill the drawer. The silverware is
monogrammed with an S on each piece.

The S stands for Stachelhaus, my mom's maiden name and my
Tanta Anna's last name. Tanta Anna never married so it makes sense
that my mom inherited these pieces. Mom's brother, Peter, a pilot in
World War II crashed and died in the mountains of China. Only she
was left to inherit. No wonder she cries when Dad mocks the
monstrosity for its ugly girth. There is so much pain just in that top
drawer.

We move when I am 12. Mom finally gets her dream of a Garrison
colonial house with a front entrance. The monstrosity's veneer is
beginning to crack and lift off. But the monstrosity still moves across
town with us. Mom ignores my dad's request to "weed it out" before
the move. My mom is excellent at ignoring what she doesn't want to
do. She just nods and smiles. Her monstrosity is a vessel of love. No
weeding needed.

Thank God the monstrosity doesn't move into my bedroom this
time. I've won my whining war. Dad demotes it to the basement, next
to the washer and dryer. Mom hangs outgrown clothes on the pipes
next to it.

She cannot seem to donate anything to Goodwill. My brother and
I try to convince her to go down to the basement and sort and toss.
She's not as emotional with us, as with Dad. She aims to please. We
can do this, I bet. But there is always some logical reason why she
cannot donate anything hanging on those pipes.

"I'm saving that for Mrs. Linscog." "This might fit Carolyn Blackmar." "I thought I might wear this next spring. It's a perfectly good coat." Her voice quivers, her eyes fill, as we push a little harder but never as hard as Dad.

We don't even try to confront the monstrosity, standing behind the pipes.

She always wins the hoarding game even though Dad leans on her to "do something about the basement." He has some spiritual reason why she should weed out. "Human accumulation is not necessary. We should only accumulate spiritual ideas."

I give Mom credit for prevailing in this one teeny tiny aspect of her life. She's not interested in accumulating spiritual ideas. The magazines that house the spiritual ideas, she doesn't mind piling up in the corner of the basement.

"If only spiritual ideas could feel as important as going shopping and drinking Brigham's mocha sodas," my dad harps at her. She keeps her old friends, the coats and dresses, the silver and tablecloths safely enshrined in the drawers of the monstrosity.

Tell us more about this monstrosity, I wish I could say now.
But I'd call it a highboy.
Tell me more about yourself.

FRENZY

There is the other universe, of the heart of man that we know nothing of, that we dare not explore.

D. H. Lawrence

Leaving Pollard Junior High at 2:30, I'm poised for a fight.

My Achilles tendon tightened and ached after PE. It humiliated me to walk into the gang showers in my bare feet. There's no way I could go to a sock-hop dance on the weekend and look normal.

Like any adolescent, I had to take out my grief and exhaustion on someone. Getting into the tan dented Dodge Dart, I avoided the front seat. I didn't want to be my mom's companion. No, just get me home so I can slam the door to my bedroom.

"How was your day?" she chirped.

Always cheerful, always making me crazy with that positive attitude.

"It stunk, okay? Just drive." I used my best nasty voice.

Mom had turned off *As the World Turns* to come and get me. A labor of love. Mousy brown hair, shirtwaist dress, old brown loafers and skin cancer starting on her face. My mom was weak, a servant to my dad. She was a pleaser, always avoiding "inharmony." She ate too slowly and with her mouth open. That was my assessment as a 12-year-old.

It seemed totally logical to me to constantly be angry with her.

My convoluted logic went like this. My mom gave birth to me. It must be her fault that I was born imperfect. Like Hephaestus, the mythic god who also blamed his mother for his deformity, I wanted revenge. Hephaestus played tricks on his mother. I spouted disrespect and hatred.

As a kid it gave me a smidge of comfort to be able to blame someone. I constantly prayed to be healed of my deformity, but God never listened to me. So Mom was my rage target. Funny how my dad never took me aside and told me to knock it off when I lashed out in full throttle. But Dad and I were allies. We had similarities. Artistic, sarcastic, a pessimistic, not one to break out into song. I had to be loyal to some adult, didn't I? So I chose the one who took me to the library and did art work with me.

"You gave birth to me,. It's your fault. You heal it!" My childhood refrain only to my mother. No one explained simple biology or genetics at any point. This made sense since we did not believe in that. God, the great creator, no genetics involved.

Mom had hoped for a daughter, at least that is what she always told me. But why? She never told me why she wanted a daughter so badly. After my grandmother died, I found my mom's yellowed birth certificate in the family strong box. She was 21 when she learned that her birth mother had died shortly after giving birth. She lived all those years not knowing her mom was really her step-mom. Mom finally told David and I this sad story after the woman we thought was our grandmother died.

She hummed a tune and started to drive me home from school.

"Don't sing, your voice is horrible, you are always off-key."

"LOVE IS REFLECTED IN LOVE," she screamed, a quote from our religion's textbook.

With that she put her foot on the accelerator and drove 70-80 mph down the streets in our little town.

"What are you doing? Slow down!" Her fast acceleration jolted me.

"I come all this way to get you and you are so unpleasant. What did I do to deserve a daughter like this?"

"GRACIOUS SPIRIT DWELL WITH ME, I MYSELF WOULD GRACIOUS BE." She was screaming a verse of a hymn.

"Take it easy. OK? Slow down, you're going to hit someone." I saw the trees flying by. We careened past Beaufort St. Her foot heavy on the accelerator.

"Stop it, you're scaring me." What had I done?

"You make my life miserable." Mom was crying, sobbing, screeching, gulping for air.

I made *her* miserable?

I held on to the back seat armrest as she turned corners without stopping or looking. No police anywhere. Thank God there were no pedestrians crossing the street or school children walking home in the road.

Rounding the corner to Hazelton Avenue, she lurched into the driveway. She continued to sob loudly.

"What's YOUR problem?" I was the tough one. But I was scared to death. Not just that we could have killed someone. I was suddenly worried what would happen when Dad got home? Worried about his response to me, not the anguish I caused my mother.

"You're crazy!" But I was not so sure.

Maybe *I* was crazy. Why couldn't I be civil?

There was no one to talk to about it. I hurried upstairs to my room. I threw my stuffed book bag on my twin bed. I could hear her sobbing in the kitchen. I kicked off my shoes and tried to start my homework. My head pounded. I kept reliving that ride home. She never went crazy like that in front of my dad. And this was not the first time.

My mom never even talked back to him when he picked on her, so I doubt she'd have ever wanted to show him how powerful she really was, if only behind the wheel of a car.

My mom got back in the car and screeched out of the driveway. If she crashed, it would be my fault. What did the neighbors think? I bet if our family drank, she would have been an alcoholic to dull her pain. I know I would have been. We weren't allowed to smoke, or swear, or drink. What was there to do besides drive like a killer and rage?

She made it home from errands in an hour. This time the car slid quietly into the driveway. Dad drove into the garage around 5 pm. I heard them talking in the kitchen. She cried quietly to him, but I heard.

He walked up the staircase to my bedroom sighing. "Why do you need to make your mother so unhappy? She does nothing but love you."

I passively sat on my bed and watched his lips move. He never dragged me down the stairs to apologize. He never asked me what had made me so upset that day in particular. He was above talking about the "human condition." That's what we called it. A condition to overcome. How do you overcome being human? I didn't have a clue.

In hindsight I should have said, "I am so sorry. I have so much anger." Maybe I should have said, "Let's talk about that operation I need." The one he threatened when I questioned God's love for me. But I didn't know how to say what I needed. We were supposed to be complete. We had no needs. God made us that way. That's what I was supposed to declare to myself.

Did he know Mom had a crazy streak or was grief-stricken or both? Did he not know I was the same? Did he know Mom and I were a dangerous pair together, making each other so miserable?

"She gave birth to me." What a stupid statement. Why didn't he ever defend her and say my birth defect was not her fault? He always stayed in the religious mode.

"Perfect God, Perfect man." I was sick of these platitudes. I'd heard them all.

Sometimes in my bed at night, I imagined sitting in one of their laps and crying while we had a heart-to-heart. If my parents didn't comfort me, I felt justified getting back at them. My father intimidated me, so cold and cutting, yet calm and ultra-reasonable. But my mother had the softest heart. I got a reaction out of her easily. It gave me momentary solace. But how to grab the solace I really needed? Compassion, acknowledgment of my physical pain, a game plan.

Mom drove like that more than once. During one episode David was in the car with me. Years later he explained that I "provoked" Mom with my snide behavior.

Now so many decades later, I can finally reflect on my mom's driving frenzy. I think our dysfunctional give-and-take was like a dance between us. It has taken me all this time to peel back the layers of our relationship and I may not be done yet. Reflecting on "discordant" incidents is a skill I've not totally mastered. I was taught they were "error" and needed to be healed, not figured out.

Seven years later, my grandmother, my mom's stepmother, lived with us for a bit. She became very ill and an ambulance rushed her to our local hospital. Soon after, I heard my mom's distraught crying from the top of the stairs. For some reason this time I saw her as a person. She was not just my mom who gave birth to a defective me. I understood a tiny part of her at that moment. I related to the real grief and distraught crying. I finally felt a tinge of commonality. We both lived with broken hearts. I ran down to our kitchen and put my arms around her and comforted her.

Like a fairy tale, my feud with her ended that day. She broke the spell when she expressed grief for the second mother she had lost. Finally someone in the family had a human emotion connected to a real event. I had never thought Mom and I were in synch. We couldn't enjoy each other's company for so many years. Actually all along we were in synch as repressed women warriors. We didn't know the term "patriarchy." I was fighting the patriarchy of my religion's strict rules on spiritual healing. She was grieving the patriarchy that limited her ability to speak up and voice her grief over the loss of her brother, her birth mother, and her ideal me.

God was supposed to be "our best, our ever friend." That's what a hymn I sang always promised. But Mom and I needed more than God. Mom showed me, in more ways than one, how life can be destroyed by continual invisibility, and submission. My gift to her and my apology for my behavior is to aim to be visible and dogma-free.

PART II

THE DAUGHTER

PERFECT GOD, PERFECT MAN, AND THE FACE

We were refugees held captive for too long in an orthodoxy that had become a windowless room of repression and restraint.

Terry Tempest Williams

The first year of your illness you walked around town without a Band-aid on your nose. You kept teaching nursery school and Sunday school like nothing was out of the ordinary.

You embarrassed me. Junior high friends started asking me what was wrong with your nose. They saw you shopping downtown on weekends. But you and Dad didn't explain anything to David or I. Obviously something was wrong, more than an open blemish on your nose. It didn't heal, and you hadn't bumped into anything. I could never explain to friends. I nervously moved away from anyone who questioned me about your condition. I answered vacantly "nothing" if they asked what was wrong with you. I felt my voice echo, and I became numb, as I searched for anything to say that made sense.

We sat at the dinner table eating our chicken breasts and cranberry sauce. It was pretty quiet unless Dad talked about his job, or Walter Cronkite reported on the Vietnam War on the evening news. I shouldn't have been surprised. Difficult subjects were never discussed. Physical "problems" were always unreal. An "error" about God's man. "Perfect God, Perfect Man," a phrase thrown out in conversations.

I lived alone with the obvious reality of my feet. A haunting dichotomy. I'm perfect, but my feet are deformed. Which is it? Now you looked miserable, too. Our religious teachings became difficult to live, when our bodies energetically rebelled year after year. I often pondered how easy it might be to be a Christian Scientist if ailments seemed run of the mill or dissipated automatically with time. The common cold or a sprain, for instance.

I consistently asked to be excused from the dinner table as soon as I could. I put on my game face, as surly as it was, but I wanted to scream, "Put on a Band-aid!" An invisible wall prevented common sense from seeping into our home.

I never invited anyone home. Our house became off limits. And to make life more miserable, I hated being an only child.

David had left for prep school in Missouri. You couldn't get him to do his homework. A genius underachiever. So you both copped out by sending him to a Christian Science high school in St. Louis, where study halls couldn't be ignored.

Did his leaving make you ill? You two were so close. You loved his tales of decorating the gym for dances and escapades downtown after school with his latest blond girlfriend. You ironed his tan chinos every afternoon as he pilfered in the refrigerator for a snack. He was your "Dave."

Whenever those airmail letters arrived from David, you read them over and over. You folded them like a precious valentine and kept them in your purse. I imagined you reading them yet again as you sipped your daily Brigham's mocha soda downtown.

He called on Sunday afternoons when the rates were cheaper. Your voice trembled as he said goodbye. Then you cried when he hung up. You counted the days until he came home for every vacation. You planned special meals to cook for him weeks in advance.

Were you afraid he wouldn't come home like your brother who went off to war? David was at a posh prep school, not piloting a plane in World War II like Peter.

Perhaps he took a piece of you when he left. I'm certain Peter did. We never discussed the horror of that telegram telling your family they'd found his body and his crashed plane.

A piece of you. Now I wonder if there was some dark serendipity that your cancer started after David left. Maybe the accumulation of losses became too much to bear. Loss of your birth mom, loss of truth telling about when she died. Maybe loss of trust in your dad, concealing that your "mom" was your step-mom all those years. Loss of your dream of college and becoming a teacher. Your dad said a "girl" didn't need extra schooling after high school. Then there's the loss of the ideal dancing dream daughter. The loss of David to school in Missouri. Worst of all, the loss of any self-worth through Dad's constant belittling comments.

Now your losses were physically appearing as your face started disintegrating.

I kept hoping somehow we'd finally see a healing in our house. That would have been life-changing. Maybe it's the inspiration I needed to heal my feet.

Lorraine Grant, your boss, said your face scared the children in your preschool class. You still refused to wear a bandage. I heard you and Dad squabbling about it in the living room one night. Dad thought you should wear one. Usually his word became the family law. You resigned from the preschool in June. Then you couldn't teach Sunday school anymore to the 2-year-olds at the Mother Church. You, who were famous for being a wizard with toddlers. I understood that little children scare easily. I was scared to death and I was 12. The church didn't even want ushers to wear glasses in those days. Now your favorite Sunday activity was gone.

A visit to a doctor might have made sense. The area on your nose refused to heal. It began to spread. Your Christian Science friends were silent, of course. For a religion based on God's love for man, I rarely detected human love "being made manifest" to our family during your illness.

David came home for Christmas break and Dad's parents came up to visit from New Jersey. David and Pop Pop shared the same birthday, December 28th. I baked a chocolate birthday cake from scratch and started frosting it with buttercream.

Suddenly the blinking lights of the police car lit up the driveway. A policeman came to the side door with you. You looked shook up. Your chin was bandaged. The policeman told David and I you'd totaled the Rambler. Just then, Dad arrived home from work in Boston and pulled up next to the police car. The policeman, you, and Dad came into the kitchen to get out of the snow.

The policeman told us it looked like you needed stitches. We had no doctor, where would she go for stitches? Our Rambler, towed to some body shop, never seen again. Dad and you rushed out the door into the blowing snow. We had no idea where you were going. In our house we didn't cry and carry on. We knew who was in control, God. But it felt like everything was out of control.

I finished frosting the chocolate birthday cake but my heart was racing. I made sure the birthday pork roast wasn't burning. David sat silently on the yellow kitchen chair, looking at the faded plastic wall clock. This was your second totaled car. It always occurred around this time of year. Was it the snow and ice in New England? What distracted you? Then I remembered you told me your brother's plane went missing at Christmas time. They didn't find his body for five months.

The grandparents sat silently on the couch in the living room with the lights off. I peeked in. That's what we called them, "the grandparents." They must have been praying. *I'd better not disturb them,* I thought.

You came back about an hour later with stitches on your chin but no Band-aid on your nose. Dad took your coat to hang up. Where did you find a doctor just like that? Dad had names of doctors just in case? I could feel the tension in that kitchen as you walked in, not explaining a thing.

I asked Dad why you had stitches one place but not the other. The air froze. He turned bright red. I figured if you could sew up a chin, you could sew up a nose. I was only 12 and that seemed logical to me.

Dad looked at me and snapped, "Shut up!"

As mad as he'd been with me before, he'd never told to me to shut up. Then he added, "You don't know a thing about this."

"I'm just asking a question."

As I ran up the stairs, David peeked his head out of his bedroom. "What's going on?"

I told him Dad had just told me to shut up. Me and my big mouth.

I needed to talk to someone badly. I needed someone to tell me I was not crazy, or alone, or in danger.

Maybe Mrs. Reading, a Christian Science practitioner, who healed spiritually was home. I closed the master bedroom door and dialed the memorized number, 444-5509. When Mrs. Reading answered, I couldn't stop sobbing. I couldn't even get my name out. But she knew my sob, for frustrated sobbing was part of my visit in her home office each Friday. You and Dad both thought something was wrong with me besides my feet. You said it was my "disposition." I was sure you two needed weekly visits, not just me.

I mean who was screwed up in this family? You, me, or all of us?

I felt comfortable telling her on the phone about your accident that evening and you getting stitches on your chin but not your nose. But there was no comfort in this phone call. There was no way to get this practitioner to talk about real people and real problems. She stayed in the spiritual realm. That night frustrated me, just as my day-to-day living caused me to question my faith, and worst of all, sanity.

As I started to write this, I realized I still believed the doctor ignored your nose and just fixed your chin. But maybe the doctor knew it was cancer and told you to find a good doctor.

Dad would never have told me that. Naively, I thought a stitch or two on the nose could cure that blemish. Maybe that is why Dad said I didn't know anything about it. Because I didn't. And no one clued me in. It would have been scary hearing the word *cancer*, but it was just as troubling not hearing anything. As a result, my imagination ran wild. I was always sure you were just about to die.

God was never in control at our house, just fear.

I don't remember what that December birthday dinner was like. Knowing us, we probably ate the tender pork roast and the frosted cake like nothing had happened, in silence.

Dad never apologized to me for telling me to shut up. I couldn't call any of my friends from school and bitch about it, because they'd never understand what I was talking about.

Healing? Relying on God? One stitched body part and one not? That night permanently informed me of my status in our family. SHUT UP. And I got the silent treatment from Dad for a day or two.

I just stared straight ahead and separated myself from reality. Why didn't I ask you about it? But I never did, not for the next 17 years while I watched you deteriorate. Without a doctor, but finally a bandage.

When it progressed so that you couldn't bandage yourself anymore, a Christian Science nurse came to our house. She cleaned the spreading wound and bandaged behind closed doors in your bedroom. I stayed in my bedroom trying to hear what you two talked about. I couldn't detect a thing.

The nurse left with no discussion. Her only job was to meet your "human need," not discuss how the disease was progressing. She was to deny the "physical senses." That's what a Christian Science nurse does. When the nurse left, I always wanted to ask you if it hurt to have the wound cleansed, if it was getting worse, if you were scared. I wanted to tell you how scared I was but didn't want to upset you when you had so much of your own horror going on.

All through the years my confusion just kept growing. Panic was a natural state.

Our rally cry was, "Only through radical reliance on Truth can scientific healing power be realized." That left us with very little wiggle room.

I sat in high school and junior high trying to concentrate on my classes, but thinking about losing you. Forcing myself out of the fear realm and into the classroom took discipline.

In college I was scared you'd come visit with your face disintegrating. What would my friends think? What would I say? Yes, they were all the same religion as me, but no one else's parent had their face covered like you.

My friends were so excited when their parents came to campus for Thanksgiving. David and I were terrified of the visit. We talked about it once in the concourse before you and Dad arrived. My heart was racing the whole time we ate turkey in the school dining room. Of course, no one mentioned your face, but everyone noticed. Friends and their parents scattered as we went through the buffet line. That's the irony of the religion. Deny the reality of a disease but run like hell. Now you see it, now you don't?

Where was my compassion? Mostly I felt embarrassment, and only a little compassion. And so much fear for my future—and yours.

How did other people cope with big problems and impending death?

VALET OF MISERY

Valet of misery,
Taking those brown oxfords to the basement
Each night to polish and buff.
Somehow make them palatable
To assuage the guilt.

Shoetrees trying to reshape the deformity.
Each time I looked at those feet
They disgusted me.
Which ridiculous socks or tights will I wear?

I mocked myself for all of them.
It saved time.
But perhaps, I, too, was a valet of misery.

Wasn't I the one who brought ice cream and socks
To that room where neither could be enjoyed?
Pretending my errands brought relief,
When really nothing could.

THE ARCHITECTURE OF HEALING

There's nothing worse than meaningless pain and meaningless suffering.
Marion Woodman

Taking my mother to the B.A. (formally called the Christian Science Benevolent Association) was like committing a loved one to a tomb while still alive. That's how I felt that Columbus Day in 1980 and long before then. The skin cancer on her face started in 1962. By 1980 my mom could not see well enough for my dad to care for her.

When I was a child, if a family friend was "at the B.A.," it was whispered about. The B.A. is supposed to be a place of "refuge and healing," But too many of our family friends went there and never came out. When I asked why, my father always said, "They waited too long" or "They let it go too far." How do you know when you've waited too long for God to heal you? And how can you tell if the disease has gone too far, when we never went to a doctor for a diagnosis?

Dad's statements seemed as dark as the architecture of the building housing all this "healing."

I knew just where it was located on Rt. 9. We drove past it every Sunday on the way to church. The black and gold sign on the right side of the highway read, "Christian Science Benevolent Association." It was up a steep, winding hill.

I saw the castle like architecture from the back seat of the car. "That place is so spooky." I said. "Don't take me there if I get sick."

My father always corrected my incorrect thinking. "Many wonderful healings have happened there. "

"Who got healed?" I sincerely wanted to know. He never gave me specific names. I had a premonition of doom every time we drove by that gold sign.

Now years later, we drove up the driveway to the B.A. with my mom in the front seat. My stomach churned and my heart sank with grief.

At 30, my fears about walking in to the B.A. came true that fall afternoon, but I couldn't crumble. I was the "strong" one.

I tried to keep up my perky banter, but I felt sick. My job was to maintain the facade of this being one more step in my mom's healing. The nurses and my dad appeared so cheerful as they unpacked Mom's blue Samsonite suitcase. Mom sat on the bed expressionless.

Mom lived in the B.A. for thirteen months.

Each Friday I drove an hour down to our family home from Boxford, where I taught. I stayed the night with Dad. I visited Mom Friday nights and Saturday afternoons. I did the grocery shopping for Dad Saturday mornings, and bought prepared meals that Dad could make on his own.

I had been coming home every weekend for five years before this. I'm sure some of my feelings of responsibility for my mom's care came from the way we had never gotten along until I was about 20. I felt like I had to make up for the lost time. I also had such pity for the life she was leading.

I tried to make up for that by doing errands, making dinners, and telling her about my kindergarten students on the weekends. She'd wanted to be a kindergarten teacher. Mom loved to hear what songs I was teaching them, what art projects the children created, and how my observations from the superintendent were going. She knew I had fought long and hard to get a job. She remembered how some superintendents asked if I'd be able to keep up with the students with my feet. This job I finally got was a major victory. She delighted in my being back in Massachusetts after three years in California.

I had no social life anyway, so weekends at Mom and Dad's filled the days. But the house was a hollow shell without my mom.

Each Friday night, the man at the side desk in the entrance to the B.A. took the payment for the week. He smiled like I was paying a restaurant tab. I never made eye contact. I wanted to yell, "Do you know what is happening? My mom is dying upstairs."

I passed the ancient living room where an elderly woman was playing hymns on the grand piano. The smell of old pot roast and stale air enveloped me. In the winter, the oriental rugs drank up the slush from my sneakers. I headed quickly to the elevator.

Up the elevator to the second floor and the smell of sickness and death. Maybe I just imagined that each week. I felt like I was on a private deathwatch. I walked past my mom's room to check in at the nursing station. I heard the humming of the electric air purifier coming from room number 224, from her room.

I was allowed to enter room 224 if no nurse was tending to Mom. The nurses changed her bandage and helped her shower each day. They cleaned her up after meals and took her to her private bathroom. After checking in, I tiptoed down the hall and knocked on her door.

Mom expected me. I always arrived with some kind of care package. I tried to vary the offerings with her favorites: mocha chip ice cream from Bergson's, panty hose from Woolworth's, a smaller size of underwear, and of course, multiple boxes of the softest Kleenex. I hoped these gifts would make up for the solitude she endured during the week. I sat on her bed next to her.

She held my hand.

Each week I felt my stomach drop to my feet when I saw the progression of the disease. The bandages had gone from covering her nose, to her nose and one side of her face, and then to her eye. It looked like her upper lip would need to be bandaged next.

I kept wondering, when was enough, enough?

I tried to deny my negative thoughts. I tried not to dwell on how she looked. I knew I was not helping the healing. I lingered outside Mom's door after saying goodbye each week. I hoped she'd still be alive the next Friday.

I stifled tears until I drove down the steep driveway. Then I sobbed for the first half-hour home on Rt. 95. The second half of the trip my mind went numb. I drove into my apartment driveway not remembering how I got home. I lay on the couch in a drained stupor until darkness.

I called my mom each night before I went to bed. She begged me not to hang up. She was now the child, and I was supposed to be the soothing mother. I read hymns to her until she calmed down.

Then it took me hours to fall asleep. All night I heard her childlike, frightened voice in my head. The hymns did not have the calming influence they once had on me. My stomach lurched. If only I could demonstrate what the hymns promised, healing.

David lived in Michigan with his first wife. I had the time to give to Mom.

All of the patients on the second floor of the B.A. were relying exclusively on "God's power" for healing. That meant there was no pain medication, antibiotics, no intravenous feeding. The bed was a "hospital" bed but its only function was to prop a head up or lay it down. There was a call button in case she needed help getting to the bathroom.

I had to numb my feelings and pretend this was fiction. I had to steel myself for the "testimony of the material senses," which I had learned was false. Mom's situation seemed so real. She could hardly talk anymore. When she ate, the food ran out of her destroyed mouth onto her blue bib.

My mom was not allowed to attend communal hymn sings in the living room downstairs. They told my dad it might "disturb the others who were seeking healing." She was never allowed to leave her room. It greatly disturbed me that she was virtually a prisoner. The hymns and Sunday service were pumped into her room by loudspeaker. She lay there alone.

My father told me sometimes nurses left her room and cried. They found it "difficult." That was an understatement. The "skilled care" they provided, that is, bandaging, only went so far. It was not the nurses' fault. It's the only service they were trained to do

The stench was overwhelming. I started bringing three air fresheners to her room each week. The electric air purifier never made a dent. I'm not sure if Mom could smell her own room. We never talked about the smell. That would have made her condition a "reality."

Sometimes the urge to fall to the ground and scream enveloped me. But I'd learned to control myself even in impossible situations. I was supposed to act steadfast in my faith in God. No wailing allowed.

The head nurse wanted me to bring mom some beef bone broth. She felt Mom was not getting enough nutrition. Obviously. But since we didn't have an IV for beef bone broth, how would it go into her mouth and belly and stay there? How many calories could beef bone broth possibly have? I was already having trouble finding underpants small enough for her. She was clearly losing weight each week. Was God her sustenance or was food or neither?

I was getting more and more confused, desperate, and depressed. I made her a gallon of beef bone broth from steak meat and brought it over whenever the nurse requested.

I felt like I was losing my mind, my heart, and my mother. Could I be the only one who knew how this would end? Why didn't anyone else notice or step in to save her? It seemed to me that Mom was being abused and neglected. Her agony, so obvious, her solitary confinement, extreme. If they could not help her, despite their healing expertise, was it not the responsibility of someone to get her medical help? That someone: Should it have been my dad, or my brother, or me? It's a question I have to live with.

I tried to bring solace any way I could. I decorated her room with leaf motifs in the fall. I scoured church fairs for a fabric Christmas tree that fit on her dresser in December. When Mother's Day rolled around, I bought the smallest pastel sweater I could find.

My father relied on my brother and me for support and help. He rarely asked for help from any church friends although they knew she was in the B.A. Word travels fast in our small religious community. Of course if we reached out, we might be suspected of not acknowledging our "victory over the five physical senses." We might look like our hearts were breaking rather than knowing that "man lives and moves and has his being with God." So we shouldered the burden alone.

I couldn't tell any of my teacher friends where I went every weekend. They wouldn't believe that I was watching my mother die without medical care. I didn't tell my Christian Science friends either. I didn't want to make a reality out of error.

I kept wondering if this was really the way Mom wanted to end her life. Maybe my thinking was not helping her healing. I wondered if Dad had asked her recently if she wanted to go home and pass on there or go to a hospital, however late it was? I wonder why didn't I ask that? What percentage of the blame is mine?

She continued to call her practitioners daily. In fact by the time she died, their numbers were on auto dial. That's not a joke. It haunts me that she did not live one day for 19 years without physical pain.

When I visited, she'd never talk about pain. But it frightened me like a monster ready to devour. She winced and cried out, but then she asked about what I was teaching at school, how was David's job, and when Dad would visit next?

Mom told me about the nurses she loved and all about their families. I heard my father admonish her to "pay attention to what is important." It sounded cruel to me. He got to stand up and walk out of her stinking room each week. I wondered if my mom felt betrayed by her practitioners and her family members, who kept telling her what to do and how to think.

As a teenager, I heard her once telling my dad she wanted to go to a doctor. She cried, "I can't take this anymore." She wept and sounded desperate. I had momentary hope for her relief. But I should have known better.

My dad said it would be wrong to get a diagnosis. He asked Mom, "Do you really want to open yourself up to that?" She backed down. She was alone with her anguish.

Why didn't I run downstairs and say, "I will take you. I will help you?" *What was I thinking* to just hide behind my closed door?

She died October 14, 1981. She couldn't breathe. There was no oxygen in her room in more ways than one.

THE CHILL IN THE AIR

The price of obedience has become too high.
Terry Tempest Williams

Thirty-eight years later it is the same October sky, the same chill in the air, the same swirling leaves. I feel it coming each year. I wait for October and start thinking, "Oh, it still feels like summer, not like when Mom died." But then, by the next week it begins.

I had visited Mom during Columbus Day weekend, and I knew this time, and *really* this time, she was nearing the end. I'd felt that way for years. I'd wonder, "Will she be alive this Christmas?" But this time, I could answer the Christmas question with a "no."

As I walked in her room that day she was lying in bed mumbling about going home soon. Mom talked about seeing her mom. "Hi Mommy," she said to me. She repeated herself and sometimes called out in pain. Her breathing was erratic. I sat next to her holding her tiny hand. The wedding rings on her fingers were too loose. I was afraid they'd come off in her bed.

I talked about nothing. My voice sounded hollow. I'd never sat with a dying person before. I'd only do this for Mom. I'm a total coward. I couldn't stand to even see a dead bird on the sidewalk.

Mom's skin shone translucent and waxy. I could see every vein in her hand. The room was eerily still. No nurse knocked on the door during my visit.

Outside the blazing sun had been replaced by an overcast sky. The huge oak trees out her window were swaying. The yellow leaves were gently falling, but when a gust of wind blew, they swirled frantically. It's the season to let go. I didn't want my mom to ever let go.

I came back the next day. I'm not sure she knew I was there. She could barely breathe. I knew this was the day for the final goodbye. She had stopped talking. The one eye she could barely see out of was closed. There was no more talk of "going home."

I sat in the silence with her. I told her what a good mom she'd been. How everyone loved her. How I hoped she got to see her brother and her mom. I told her she was safe and could just let go, that we'd be okay.

I didn't really think I'd ever be okay again, but I had read books about dying and they said to tell the dying we'd be okay. I stood back and watched her for a few minutes. Her eensy little body hardly made a lump in the bed. I stood up and faced her.

I always thought Dad would die first. He seemed the most sensitive and dramatic. The most frail. But here was this warrior. Nineteen years of diseased torture. I walked closer to the bed and put my hand on her head. I stroked her feathery gray hair. I told her everything was okay. I told her I loved her so much. Then I closed her door and tiptoed out to the hall. It was empty. I made it to the elevator and out the door to my car. I just sat there and sobbed.

Finally I drove the hour back home to my Newburyport apartment, blowing my nose and wailing. I sat in the driveway watching those leaves swirl and the sky darken.

I called David and asked if he was going to see Mom. "Get over there, the end is really close." It scared him to be alone with her. But he promised he'd go. David would drive my dad over with him, I was sure.

Wednesday after teaching, I immediately drove home to my apartment. I called Mom the instant I got in the door. I knew she wouldn't be able to talk, but a nurse could hold the phone to her ear. I was going to say hi, go walk the dog, and then drive down to see her again. When I asked for her room number, the switchboard transferred me to the nurse's station.

The head nurse got on the phone and said, "Mrs. Cook is having trouble breathing. She can't talk right now."

"Can you put the phone up to her ear? It's her daughter." She said it wasn't possible.

I hung up abruptly and called Dad. "Should I rush down? I can leave now."

He said, "No, the end is near."

"Why aren't you with her?" He calmly told me a coworker offered to give him a ride home.

"WHAT????" I yelled and started to cry.

He told me to stop crying.

I called David. "Did you know he left Mom to die alone?"

David said he'd go right over to Dad's and drive him to Mom's bedside. Before another minute passed, my dad called back and said Mom had just died.

I yelled into the phone, "Alone? Alone? Why didn't anyone call me this morning?"

"Oh, her favorite nurse was with her. The nurses will bathe her before the undertaker comes."

"After all she gave for us, you couldn't sit with her?"

It was like Jesus being betrayed by Judas.

I raced to my car. The moon was full. The leaves were swirling. October 14th is always the same.

EITHER HERE OR HEREAFTER

Foundations of identity tremble when the edifice is shaken.
Ginette Paris

Mom died around 4:30 pm.

I frantically drove to our family home in the early October darkness. The moon was full. I kept blowing my nose and throwing the Kleenexes on the floor of my Honda. My green backpack was full of random clothing I grabbed out of my bedroom dresser. I drove into the driveway of my parents' house. In the old days the light post was lit and Mom watched from the window to see me pull in.

That would never happen again.

I didn't call any of my teaching colleagues. My mom's illness was a secret. I used to tell them I went down to my parents' house each weekend to help out. I couldn't explain more. My job all along had been to "unsee" her cancer. If anyone could do that, she'd be healed. I needed to "contribute" to that spiritual frame of mind.

I heard the surprise in my principal's voice when I called and said I'd need some days off "because my mom just died." I had never told him why I raced out of the building on Fridays, why I went directly to their house to do the shopping, cleaning and banking each weekend for the last five years she was alive.

I saw David's Gremlin in the driveway. I unlocked the kitchen door. Dad and David sat numbly in the living room. David's eyes were red. Dad stared straight ahead. I stood at a distance in the entrance to the living room. Only Mom was a hugger, so we were left holding in all our grief.

I asked David what we needed to do first. I thought I might throw up from the tension and shock. It had finally happened. The funeral home needed clothes to dress mom for her cremation. I found some new underwear in her dresser. I found her favorite aqua polyester dress in her stuffed closet. Everything would be multiple sizes too big now. My hands had been shaking on the drive down. Now they were freezing cold.

I put her clothes in a brown paper bag. David drove it to the undertaker back in Boston about a half hour away. Christian Scientists use undertakers "friendly" to the religion. I was never sure what that meant. Maybe they wouldn't judge the condition of the bodies that had never had medical treatment. The undertaker had picked up Mom's body from the B.A. about an hour before. Somehow we found out the undertaker couldn't believe she had lived as long as she had in her condition. Small comfort.

I asked Dad if he needed dinner. "There's probably a Stouffer's I could heat up for you," I offered.

"No thanks, honey." He didn't look up. Maybe he was praying. Maybe he was grief stricken. With Dad it was hard to tell.

The doorbell rang and Riley, the man who drove my dad to work each day appeared with his wife. She had a foil-wrapped coffee cake in her hands. She hugged me. I couldn't let myself cry. Riley hugged me, too. I was on the edge of a full-blown sob but I held my breath and tried to concentrate on being numb. I was used to pretending that anything horrible was "fiction." There had been lots of horrible sights lately.

Dad finally came into the kitchen and we stood awkwardly, not knowing what to say to our friends. They left pretty quickly but said to call if we needed anything at all. I shoved the coffee cake in the freezer. No one had an appetite. Maybe in the morning the coffee cake would look appealing.

I went upstairs and called my mom's practitioner. She was probably one of the last people to see Mom alive or to hear about her deteriorating condition from the B. A. The person who prayed for her healing. She knew the unreality of disease.

Her husband answered right away and said, "Donna is at church."

"Well, it's just Peggy Cook, and I wanted to speak to her."

His voice had a little catch to it. He must have heard our last name before.

I sat on my parents' double bed. The white chenille bedspread was perfect for fingering and pulling threads out. Penny, my mom's schnauzer, came in. She trotted to the connecting bathroom and sniffed around.

"Are you looking for Mommy?" She stared at me, ears perking up. Then she sat glumly against my leg and sighed.

At 9:00 I thought Donna might be home from the Wednesday testimony meeting. At the end of every Wednesday night service, members stand up and testify to God's healing power. I wondered how she felt sitting there that night.

I hit the buttons on the tan princess phone. This time she picked up.

"Oh dear one," she said.

I hate that phrase. Like she was someone I knew well, an aunt or grandmother.

Mom's death was not really Donna's fault. Why did we expect a normal human to heal something that only Jesus could?

I sobbed, "At least she's not in pain anymore."

But then, Donna didn't readily agree. "Well," she began...

"What? She can't still be in pain, can she?"

"Well you know either here or hereafter she has to see the unreality of disease."

"Yah, well, she must have by now, right?" She had been dead five hours.

"The belief in sin is punished as long as the belief lasts." She was quoting Mary Baker Eddy's words from *Science and Health*.

"I don't want to believe that."

Suddenly the bedroom had a freezing chill. I had to hang up fast. Death is unreal. Disease is unreal. But you can suffer after something that didn't even happen. I'd never thought of this, but I knew that somehow there was a sick cruelty to all this. If our religion thought she was still trying to finagle a healing, fine. Other religions and schools of thought believed she was free, from October 14th, 1981 to eternity.

That's what I chose to believe.

I didn't debate the phone call with my dad. He sat on the yellow couch, speechless still. My brother sat at the den's desk, writing Mom's obituary. I didn't bother him.

I walked the dog. Then I went into my dark bedroom to get undressed for bed. Mom's gone, Mom's gone. I kept going over the last time I saw her. So waxy-looking, so tiny.

As my dad came up the steps to his bedroom, he called through the bannister, "Good night, Peg." I just couldn't go out to hug him.

My head was pounding, my eyes almost swollen shut, as the wind threw the leaves against my window all night.

The next morning Dad told us he didn't want a plot for Mom in any cemetery. We'd just scatter her ashes.

"Her ashes are not who she was." He reiterated what we had heard all our lives in church.

But I needed to know where she was. I couldn't stop crying, begging him to let me bury her ashes.

David finally said, "Let Peg give Mom a plot if it means something to her."

A cemetery representative helped David and I pick out a plot later that day at Mt. Auburn cemetery, all the way in Cambridge. Since our "leader" was entombed there, my father considered the cemetery "friendly" to Christian Science. Azalea Path. Mom loved azaleas. The plot was not too near the road. I didn't want anyone stepping on her. I chose a double plot in case we wanted to visit Dad someday, too.

I hoped she already rested easy somewhere else. Maybe she had met the birth mother she never knew. I imagine she saw her brother and gave him a long overdue hug. I hope she saw her dad, Gustav, who said, "Dottie" with that German accent. I bet her beloved Tanta Anna greeted her too.

I want to be laid to rest.

Not in isolation, please. I want my battles and joys celebrated by my family and friends that outlive me. As the song by Kenny Loggins says, "Please celebrate me home."

CELEBRATE ME HOME

We didn't have a ceremony laying my mother to rest. We refused to "glorify" death or make a "reality" of it. We didn't purchase an urn. A cardboard box held her ashes. The founder of our religion was buried in Mt. Auburn in an ornate marble vault, no cardboard box for her.

We had no funeral or memorial service. No organ music or comforting hymns. No eulogy or funny stories. No Bible verses or refreshments. We remained silent about her many years of dedicated motherhood, her passion for teaching preschoolers, and her loving generosity. We knew death wasn't real.

I believe now, though, we were afraid to lay her to rest.

This can happen to you.

The cemetery staff buried her ashes and we were absent. I read recently that the author Terry Tempest Williams waited in an adjacent room when her brother was cremated. We'd never do that. We were never a gutsy bunch.

If we had decided to have a funeral, I imagined a long line during the viewing. Mom had lots of friends, from Brigham's ice cream store, American Beauty hair salon, Eadie's Lobster restaurant, and Rimelee's fish store. She knew all the clerks' names. She brought all her favorite store owners homemade shortbread at Christmas time. Our neighbors loved her too. They'd surely have come to her funeral. Most likely her Christian Science friends wouldn't have attended her funeral. They didn't visit her when she was sick. Not one. They didn't call the whole time she was in the sanatorium. But then again, a funeral seemed neat and tidy. No bandages, or deteriorating, emaciated body. So maybe.

I think we anticipated her "downtown friends" crying at her funeral. Then what would David, Dad, and I have done? Would we have stood there like brave soldiers? Or maybe our outpouring of grief would have flooded the room. If we cried, the tears would be never ending. They'd flow right out of Eaton's Funeral Home, down Highland Avenue, filling up Rosemary Lake on the edge of town.

Our emotions were barely in control just walking around our house. What could we possibly have said to explain our neglect of a treatable condition? We'd discovered death was, indeed, real.

At church, people said they were sorry about Mom's "passing." We weren't "good" Christian Scientists if we wept hysterically or collapsed in a heap. Stoicism was the norm for us, devoted to the religion. We swallowed and kept that pulsing lump in our throats pushed down.

We called that a "healing."

"They've been 'healed' of grief." *That* was a triumph. God was our joy, our comfort, our father and our mother. So we didn't lay her to rest formally. And *we* kept grieving and grieving. We didn't acknowledge publicly what she meant to us. We didn't honor how she sacrificed her life for our religion.

But our emotions were all inside our bodies.

Eating away.

I began to understand she died for him, for his job at headquarters. She died after he convinced her not to go to a doctor. I think Dad was afraid to tell the Board of Directors Mom needed medical intervention. I think he was afraid he'd be asked to step down from his position at the Mother Church. Then what? The shame. Better to look so dedicated, so trusting.

By the time my father died, my brother and I had no feelings left for him. That's what we said to each other. We did have feelings, though. We felt betrayed. We had been trained to obey and believe.

Dad's voice, often strained and fearful, but powerful in its control over us. And look what happened. We were still thinking about Mom. Every day.

When we brought up the idea of a funeral for Mom right after her death, Dad said, "Do we really want to put ourselves through that?" He hadn't attended his own mother's memorial service. Were we a loving family or heartless? Maybe we were all cowards.

I told him I didn't want to come to Needham every weekend anymore, like I did before Mom died. He said, "You won't have me around much longer."

"Was that a threat?" I asked.

He turned away and walked into another room.

We were not healed of grief.

I needed people to comfort me and tell me what Mom meant to them. Not as a spiritual idea, but as Dottie Cook, the person who always tried to be perky in spite of her pain. I wanted to honor her sacrifice with words, songs, something. Even if I sobbed, I needed to stand up and speak. I had a constant pulse in my gut.

I wanted to lay her gently down into the earth and say, "We're so sorry. What were we thinking?"

Twenty years after Mom died, Dad was bedridden at a rehab center, recovering from a massive stroke. He couldn't speak or use his right side and was already blind from untreated detached retinas. He'd be going home soon. Home would be a nursing home. His second wife divorced him twice, so he no longer had a family home.

He took a turn for the worse the afternoon before his release and the nurses moved him to a private room. They told us he didn't have long.

I visited late afternoon. Classical music played from a radio on the white nightstand. The pine trees, lush green, blew in the breezes outside his window. The rehab staff lit a white candle to send him off peacefully. His eyes were closed.

I told him, "I am here."

He didn't stir.

I held his hand. He still had my mother's graduation ring on his pinky. I still loved his hands. So delicate, soft and gentle. They painted images and typed thousands of words.

I walked out of the rehab center. It felt so strange to just say "goodbye." I used to cry saying goodbye to him when I'd leave for college or call him from California, where I first taught. But now I needed to get home to my girls.

David visited in the evening but left before Dad's last breath. Did we leave him purposely, like he did to Mom? Dad probably didn't notice we weren't there.

We had no funeral for Dad.

Strangely, the same day Dad died, his best friend Gerald did too. Gerald was one of the only friends Dad had. He was head photographer for *The Christian Science Monitor*. They had the same middle name: Noble. When they reminisced about their careers, they joked that they had dedicated their lives to a "noble" cause.

That weekend, David gave the funeral service for Gerald at Mt. Auburn Cemetery's chapel. His widow asked him to. We'd been family friends for 40 years. It was a poignant and loving eulogy. David had Dad's gift for writing and Mom's heart.

So many Christian Scientists gathered in the little chapel. Some of his friends and all his family cried. I was in awe of this public display of emotion. I thought we didn't effuse or weep in public. I pulled out a Kleenex from my coat pocket and the tears flowed. We laid Gerald to rest. That same day, all alone, Dad was interred in the Cook plot right next to Mom.

Please celebrate me home.

PART III

THE PATIENT

MATTHEW

"You're going to be an aunt!" David called from DC jubilant. The first grandchild in the family, a brand new beginning. A gift.

My brother and sister-in-law practiced Christian Science. We didn't discuss Linda's pregnancy. We prayed and declared the "spiritual nature" of the baby vs. the physical changes happening in Linda's uterus. I never asked if she had morning sickness. I had been taught to emphasize the "perfection" of the pregnancy. That only "harmony" controlled our lives, not physical symptoms. A Christian Scientist denied unpleasant symptoms as not emanating from God, therefore, unreal.

When Matt arrived, David called and said that Linda had delivered via C-section. Right away I asked, "Is he healthy? Are his feet okay?" I only wanted him NOT to have clubfeet. I wanted the 1 in 1000 bad luck chain broken with me. David reassured, "He's fine." What a relief. Finally something positive and joyous to celebrate

Our Matthew had arrived. Buoyant, the Cook family luck changed. Even though we didn't believe in luck. We believed in "God's law." When a healing occurs, at that very moment it's instantaneous and complete. I had been praying unsuccessfully for the healing of my clubfeet for 36 years.

When I had a few days off from teaching, I flew down to DC to meet Matt. What a sweet little bird. He was a scrawny little thing, with wisps of blond hair. He looked like a Cook. His mouth was often open waiting to be breastfed. Linda seldom put him down, and if she did, she had him right next to her.

I loved looking at him even from a distance.

David told me that they had just fired the Christian Science nurse they had originally hired to help with the baby. When I asked what happened, David said, "She was very unprofessional."

"What does that mean?" I blurted out.

"Well, just because she knew Mom doesn't mean she can say anything she wants."

"Like what?" I asked.

"Well, she said his feet didn't look right and they should be checked out by the doctor."

I froze. I could feel my ears ringing. "*Are* his feet okay?" Matthew had to have been examined by the doctor that delivered him. Obviously doctors and nurses had seen him.

I needed to have time with Matthew and see for myself. One morning Linda was sleeping and Matt started to cry. "I'll change him," I called out. David went to put a load of laundry in the washer.

I can still see Matthew on the changing table wearing his little white sweater and velour blue pants. I gave him a big smile and slid his mini pants down and took off his booties. Immediately I saw what I dreaded. His tiny feet turned in just like mine. If I straightened them, they went right back into that position. His little knees turned in, too.

How could this be? How could he come out of the hospital without this being detected? How could David not notice after living with me? Had doctors really not observed this defect? Why hadn't they listened to the Christian Science nurse when she said his feet were not formed correctly? So many questions that would not be appropriate to ask filled my head.

I quickly changed his diaper and put his tiny clothes back on. I looked at his innocent little face. My father once told me that clubfeet weren't hereditary. But really, what did he know? We were so sheltered in our religion. We didn't read medical journals. My dad regularly turned down the volume on any medical news on our living room tv. We didn't listen to "error." We practiced "unseeing the material."

Currently, babies born with clubfeet are seen after a week or two by a pediatric orthopedist specializing in clubfeet. The doctor molds casts to fit the infant's feet. Every week the casts are changed and are rotated out a few degrees until the feet are finally in the right position, facing forward. It is a process that takes months. Then the young child spends years wearing special shoes with a bar connecting them to keep the angle correct. Finally the child only wears the braces and bar at night. By the time the child is school age, the contraption is no longer needed. The child starts school walking normally.

Matthew was almost a month old. While playing with Matthew during that same first visit, I asked David if he needed to be followed up at the doctor's after the delivery.

David said, "No."

My stomach in knots, I didn't dare push any further.

When my dad asked about Matthew after my visit, I didn't know what to say. He hadn't seen him yet, so I said, "He is adorable." Which was so true. It wasn't my place to break the news to him.

Where was my voice? Every time I visited Matthew his feet looked the same. He walked late. He tripped on flat surfaces. He walked on his tiptoes.

I couldn't believe we were all going to relive this nightmare. I watched for three years while Matt struggled to do what other toddlers do, run, jump and walk confidently. I winced every time I saw him with his shoes off.

One day when Matt and Linda were visiting me in Newburyport, I took them to the beach on a hot July day. They still had not mentioned anything about Matt's feet to me.

Matt was walking towards the ocean barefoot when a man stopped in front of our beach towel inquired, "Oh, does your little boy have clubfeet too?"

Linda immediately yelled, "No!"

The man ignored her answer. "My son had surgery for his, and now he can walk normally." He continued on his way.

I just stared straight ahead.

Linda asked me, "Do you think he has clubfeet?"

I felt like I was in an alternate universe. I wanted to yell and say, "Of course he has clubfeet. It is so obvious." Instead I said, "Yes, I do." She didn't ask why I hadn't said anything before. She didn't ask how I knew. But later in the day Linda used my phone. She called my brother at work and told him about the man on the beach. Later in the week they had Matthew examined in Boston. David told me they were advised to begin treatment immediately.

I didn't dare ask if they agreed that medical treatment was right for Matt. I could tell by David's voice how upsetting this day had been. I never said I'd noticed it early on. I didn't ask, "How could you not know?" I only prayed that history would not repeat itself and that my nephew would get his feet corrected.

I waited to hear something, anything. We talked each weekend but my brother never mentioned Matt's diagnosis. I'm sure there were difficult discussions going on between David and Linda. How to know when the time has come for an alternative solution, when you know God is all-powerful? How to balance God's instantaneous healing vs. needing a long drawn-out orthopedic process? How to be dedicated to your church and fair to your child?

Finally one Sunday, many months later, David called. He said, "I have to tell you something. I am looking for an orthopedic surgeon for Matthew. It's not our first choice, but I can't do this again."

I burst into tears and told him to do it. I told him how proud I was of their decision. I told him Matthew deserved to have a happy childhood. By the time we hung up, David and I were both in tears. Then something surreal happened. I sat down on my couch in the living room. It was eerily quiet except for a voice. *Maybe you should get your feet corrected, too.* Suddenly a freezing cold jolt went through my body. I called David right back. I told him the bizarre thought that had just come into my head. I'd never considered anything but a spiritual healing.

I was 37.

Right away, David replied, "Go for it. I'll help you find a doctor."

THE FIRST OPINION

My body is my compass, it does not lie.

Terry Tempest Williams

When I decided I'd like clubfeet surgery, I knew I needed the operation in Washington, DC, where my brother lived. Still single, I'd need help during my recuperation. I'd be in traction and would virtually need to be waited on hand and foot. My brother and his wife offered to let me recuperate with them.

I had no idea if surgery was even a possibility for me. I called Blue Cross Blue Shield from home one afternoon and asked if they considered clubfeet surgery "cosmetic." The agent on the phone responded, "Are you kidding?"

I'd never had health insurance even though my school system offered it. I'd been relying on prayer for my health my whole life. I signed up for health insurance immediately. I'd never be able to pay the hospital out of pocket for such multiple complicated procedures.

My foot pain had increasingly intensified as I aged. My back, knees, and hips ached after teaching school each day. I had to admit to myself that my prayers hadn't stopped the pain. I could barely walk in the morning. I struggled with a sense of doom.

I went home after teaching Monday through Friday and lay in bed by 6:30. On the weekends, all I could do was lie on the couch. By Friday I was in such pain, I'd often sleep on the couch, wrapped in a cozy blanket like a burrito. I just couldn't make it upstairs to my bedroom.

I didn't yet know about Motrin, elevating my feet, or ice packs.

Somehow, I had to find a surgeon I'd trust. My brother researched orthopedic surgeons in the DC area. David called me a few days later with the name of a respected pediatric orthopedic surgeon, Dr. Joel Schiffman. I nervously made an informational appointment with him during my next school break.

I hadn't been to a doctor for 32 years

How would I explain to Dr. Schiffman why I hadn't had surgery as a child? I rehearsed saying: *for three generations our family radically relied on prayer for physical healing.*

With my brain well trained by family beliefs, I didn't see myself as neglected. I was being faithful, waiting for my healing.

Yet my knees were on fire. My feet throbbed on shards of glass. Back pain from the unnatural torque of my body persisted. Teaching first grade meant getting up and down from the floor and walking all day. My feet swelled after bus and recess duty.

The recovery from possibly two clubfeet procedures scared me the most. I needed someone to help me realistically imagine the aftermath. The school nurse told me that foot surgery was bone-crunching painful. That was vivid enough for me. Reconstructing my feet at this age seemed like a frightening long shot, yet it had the potential to be a dream come true.

First I needed to research if it was even possible for an adult to have the procedures. On a child, the doctor cut the heel chord to lengthen it and reconstructed the heel on each foot. Next, a triangle wedge, to allow the foot to be rotated to the proper angle, was removed from the ankle. Then all toes were straightened and held in place with pins. Months of casts and physical therapy learning to walk was the norm. Was this the same for an adult? Was it even more complicated now that my older bones no longer had the flexibility of a child's?

I daydreamed of straight feet and heels at a right angle, fancy shoes and dancing.

At night I perseverated, as I lay awake in the dark wondering about the pain, the medicine I'd have to take, and learning to walk again. Finally I flew to DC on my next school vacation. The next day I timidly slid into the backseat of a taxi to Dr. Schiffman's office in Alexandria, Virginia. I clutched my purse, and told myself this appointment was just informational. I didn't have to commit to anything that day.

I entered the chilly waiting room with a knot lodged in my stomach. It had its own pulse. The receptionist checked me in and gave me multiple forms to fill out. I was used to privately praying for a healing at home. Now I had to publicly speak and write about my clubfeet. My voice echoed in my head as I spoke to the receptionist. I teetered on breaking down just sitting in that waiting room.

The nurse led me into the examining room full of stainless steel. I'd never willingly shown my deformed feet to anyone. I waited for Dr. Schiffman. I dangled my feet over the edge of the table like a child. He knocked on the door and came in. He introduced himself and shook my hand. He had the forms I'd filled out with him on a clipboard. I had no medical records to share, I volunteered. I quickly explained why.

He didn't seem phased. He'd performed clubfeet surgery before, he explained, just a few times but never on an adult. That frightened me. I tried not to judge.

I untied my sneakers and took off my socks. Goosebumps suddenly covered my body. There was no hiding the deformed shape of my feet from his examining eyes. My feet pointed in and faced each other. There was no heel to help me stand flat. My feet were shaped like clubs on playing cards, my toes were misshapen and deformed.

This doctor was the first person in decades to touch my feet. He lifted one forefoot up to see what kind of side-to-side movement it had. Not much. There was no up-and-down movement either. He had strong, confident hands. They were gentle and warm.

He asked if I could walk for him. I had no balance in bare feet. But I rolled up my pants' legs to prepare. He helped me off the metal table onto the cold linoleum floor.

This was the moment I dreaded. I walked my awkward, crooked gait for him in the room and then out into the hallway. I didn't try to walk "straight" like I did for family members. It felt good not to have that pressure from a doctor.

Would he look repulsed as I walked down the hall on the balls of my feet? I looked straight ahead, trying to maintain my balance. Dr. Schiffman held out his hand in case I needed help. I felt tears well up from this unexpected gesture.

"I don't know how you walk with your feet in this severe condition."

"Really?" I said, swallowing sobs.

"It is remarkable," he added. He brought a chair over for me to sit in. He was the first person to ever validate my condition. He asked what I did for a living.

"Teacher" I said.

When he heard I taught elementary school, he asked, "Aren't you in pain?"

"Every day."

"What do you take for pain?"

"Nothing."

He asked if he could ask his associate to come in. *Oh, God,* I thought, *what a freak show.* But I gave him the okay.

The next doctor came out of his office to have a look. He was equally impressed that I wasn't in a wheelchair. He asked if he could take pictures of my feet. He went to get his Polaroid.

I couldn't believe I was letting this stranger take pictures of my feet. Not feeling judged was new and strangely liberating. It wasn't my fault I was walking crooked. It was the condition. It wasn't a personal or spiritual failure as I was conditioned to feel. I wasn't guilty in this setting. When the other doctor left, I asked Dr. Schiffman if I was too old for corrective surgery. I held my breath for the answer. All of a sudden I wanted it. For sure.

He told me without hesitating that it could be done. He described procedures he would use to correct the deformities. He sounded a little too confident like it was no big deal. Maybe that was supposed to make me feel good. I took copious notes, but he said he would also mail me a written report. Then I asked him how many clubfeet patients he had treated. He said five children. My heart sank. That was not enough for me. I wanted someone who had operated on at least a hundred. He said he would do one foot and his associate would do the other at the same time.

That plan freaked me out. All I could imagine were two feet that didn't match after surgery. I was disappointed because I knew I'd have to have the surgery in DC and this person came highly recommended. Plus his kindness was an unexpected bonus.

He told me I should get a second opinion in Boston near where I lived. He knew a few names that he'd share in his report.

All in all, I walked out of that appointment feeling victorious. Not because the perfect doctor had appeared, but because I'd survived an exam. I hadn't crumbled in front of doctors. These doctors helped me feel a smidge proud for persisting all those years. They confirmed how painful clubfeet were and the normalcy of pain in other parts of the body as a result. Validation, even decades too late, felt freeing. I'd been respected and heard. I knew I was supposed to deny deformity as not real, not made by God. But this afternoon I gave myself permission to listen to the doctors instead of the religious teachings that echoed in my mind day and night.

My father had always told me that doctors were uncaring and cold. Dr. Schiffman and his partner had not fit that description at all.

Within a week I had a follow-up letter from Dr. Schiffman. The first doctor in Boston on his recommended list was on vacation when I called his office. The receptionist told me to call Dr. Seymour Zimbler. Dr. Zimbler and the vacationing doctor had once shared an office. I worked up my nerve to call him the next day.

In the meantime, I daydreamed of straight feet.

Of course at that point I'd no idea what was REALLY involved yet. But I imagined walking in beautiful shoes, running on the beach and wearing dresses. That kept my mind busy and thrilled during the day. But fear taunted me in the dark of night. How would I learn to walk again, how could I handle the pain, how would my life change? What if my life was worse after the surgery? I was used to worrying about everything, but this worrying seemed valid.

That night I couldn't sleep. I turned on Health Network. From a distance the medical world always intrigued me. I wanted to see how doctors cured physical problems. I relied on God for my health. How did people fare who didn't?

It was 3 am and on the screen "Up next: clubfeet surgery on a fetal pig." What were the chances? I moved closer to the 13-inch tv. The commercials finally ended. When I saw the doctor flip the pig on its belly and slice open its leg, I almost vomited.

I couldn't fathom doctors doing that to me. I was sure the doctors would scoff at my too fat body while I was under anesthesia.

Aghast, I clicked off the tv before the pig's feet were straightened.

DR. ZIMBLER

The desire of our hearts makes a path.

Joy Harjo

Dr. Zimbler's specialty is infants and children with cerebral palsy, spina bifida, and clubfeet. But I'm 36, not seven months old. I've heard all my life how uncaring doctors are so I am certain he won't see me. But I get up the nerve to call, sweating bullets in my bedroom. Susan, the office manager, assures me she'll ask Dr. Zimbler and get back to me. I doubt she'll ever call back. I am used to broken promises and disappointments.

Two days later, Susan calls me and says Dr. Zimbler will consult with me about the possibility of clubfeet surgery. She tells me to bring any records I have. I have no records. This statement does not faze her.

His office sends me a confirmation letter of my appointment. When I see the logo on the stationary, I love this doctor immediately. A child is throwing down crutches and jumping in the air. By the time my appointment comes around, David has been transferred from Washington, DC to Boston. What were the chances of that happening? I'd never heard the word synchronicity before. Now finding a doctor in Boston becomes important for more than just a second opinion.

I take a dry run to Newton to find his office. I have no sense of direction. But I find his small satellite office on Washington St. It is right next to Brigham's ice cream store. A good omen. His office is not in a foreboding hospital or medical building. Who would have thought I'd ever be looking for a doctor's office?

I'm easing gradually into the medical world. I peek into the door but don't go in. Now I'm mentally prepared for my appointment.

In the waiting room, infants and children are in their parents' arms or in a small, enclosed play area. Some have full leg casts or braces. I'm the only adult patient. My appointment is at 2 pm. Susan apologizes for the delay. At 3:15 my name is called. I am about to experience why I've waited so long in the waiting room.

Clutching a clipboard and pen, I walk into a tiny examining room, heart pounding, and sit on a plastic chair. I take off my shoes and socks. In here I don't have to feel self-conscious about the shape of my feet. All around me are casting materials: gauze, tape, fiberglass for molding casts, and a saw for removing casts. There is a diagram of a foot's skeletal structure hanging on the wall.

When Dr. Zimbler enters the room, I am riveted by his kind smile. He is about 60, in a grey suit, gray thinning hair, with a low, tender voice.

I tell him my story. My voice starts to shake. I might cry. He listens standing across from me making eye contact the entire time. I tell him my parents say surgery is very dangerous. The story goes that I might not walk again if the heel chord is cut incorrectly. So I never have corrective surgery growing up. I don't mention the religion yet. He asks if I recall the name of the doctor I saw in infancy for the diagnosis of clubfeet?

I remember my parents mentioning one doctor's name: Dr. Karp. Dr. Zimbler says Dr. Karp was a well-known clubfoot doctor in the 1950s. He says the surgery was not dangerous then and even less so now. But then he reassures me it's normal for parents to be fearful.

Then I tell him about my religion.

I blurt out that I am so angry that I've lived this way for so long.

He looks me in the eye and says, "Dear, we can only go from here. Let's see what we can do."

I had been told doctors were enemies of "real" healing. But this doctor is ready to move forward. He does not condemn the different strategy of healing my family practiced.

So we start. First a technician takes x-rays from all the angles of both feet. Next I walk down the linoleum hall in bare feet for Dr. Z. There are no railings. It's always difficult to keep my balance bare foot. But surprisingly I don't feel self-conscious.

I notice PTs and casting technicians looking on in this eight-room enclave. It seems like a caring community, not sterile at all. He watches carefully, pointing out to technicians what he observes about my feet. Sometimes he points at my x-rays now on the wall. He watches my knees and hips, too. Dr. Zimbler's face has no expression of judgment. He makes clinical observations about metatarsals, heel chords, angles, the degrees of my knees, and the rotation of my hips.

Hearing these physical facts brings me comfort. I'm not embarrassed about my feet anymore. He is not judging my worthiness to be healed. To Dr. Zimbler, clubfeet have nothing to do with my character.

After I sit back down in his office, he cradles each foot in his warm hands and tries to move them up and down, left to right. He takes notes.

He asks what I do for a living. He's floored that I teach young children, a job that requires standing for hours. He gives me positive feedback about my tenacity. He talks about my courage, something I'd never considered before. I'm used to soldiering on, looking as normal as I can. I don't want to lose my job over my feet. I have to be more than competent.

This appointment changes my life. I see kindness in action.

I ask if he has ever done clubfeet surgery on adults. He says he rarely takes an adult's case. It's complicated surgery at this age. He tells me about a woman from Italy that he operated on years ago. She does well until she gains too much weight. Weight adds to the burden of the corrected feet, he explains, and causes too much pressure to the feet, knees, and hips. *I need to drop some weight*, I think.

He says he'd take my case. I timidly ask how many clubfeet surgeries he does a year? I don't want to seem ungrateful, but I want someone ultra-experienced.

He says, "About 80 give or take."

I shake inside from joy and terror. I'm sure he can see my stomach doing somersaults.

"Thank you so much." My voice echoes. I'm freezing and I will my tears not to fall.

I am about to commit to something so overwhelming, but necessary. I feel too young to make this decision on my own. But I'm 37. I'm not young anymore. I'm not asking anyone's permission. My mom is dead. My dad would be horrified. He runs from anything dangerous. I saw it with Mom. Better to hang on to the familiar than search for an alternative he doesn't trust. I will tell him much later. My brother and sister-in-law will be supportive, like always.

Later I learn how upset David always was seeing me so unhappy during my childhood. I always thought he was the lucky one, unscathed by clubfeet. But now genetics has taken a turn, and Matthew will need surgery from an orthopedic surgeon, too.

I find the top doctor in the field without knowing it. Finally destiny is kicking in. Later I learn Dr. Zimbler teaches at Harvard Medical School and operates at Children's Hospital, Newton Wellesley and Beth Israel. He is the go-to doctor in the field.

He and I talk logistics. I want him to do both feet in the same time frame, so I don't miss too much teaching time. He tells me it will be 6 months to even walk again with crutches and walking casts and about a year and a half of PT. He tells me about the three months I will be in traction. I hear the words *weight bearing* for the first time. The surgery will take 7 hours per foot. That was sobering, but I didn't know how sobering yet.

He tells me he will do both feet within a week, but it is not his preference. He says the recuperation is difficult and doubly so if both feet are involved. He emphasizes I will need to learn to walk all over again with my new heels and reformed feet facing in the correct direction.

I'm adamant that I have to do this at the same time. Sometimes I don't listen to my elders. I've had to be headstrong. I will learn extreme humility in this new endeavor.

When I ask about the pain, he says, "There will be some discomfort." This is what I learn to love about him. He is the master of understatement. He uses *discomfort*, not "mortal agony." Not "you will be screaming for the morphine." Not "it won't be easy getting off the Percocet." He likes to take things step-by-step and not cause panic.

It is August and we tentatively schedule surgery for my April vacation from school. He tells me there is much to do. He wants me back for further x-rays and consultations each month. He wants me to donate my own blood for the surgery and start taking iron pills. I don't even know how to swallow pills. He'll set up a tour of the hospital to ease anxiety. I need extensive pretesting. I don't know what this means but he says he'll send a list to me and the hospital will know exactly what tests I need.

This is why his appointments take so much time. He does not rush explaining any procedures. He is not condescending. *He* asks what questions I have. Innocently I ask if someday I could maybe wear dress shoes.

Little do I know, I will be happy to get my feet in sneakers and socks again.

As I leave the office that day, Susan hands me a sheaf of papers to fill out. I look at the parents still waiting with their children for their appointments. No one looks aggravated that I've been in his office for an hour and a half.

They must know from experience their child will get just as much attention when their time comes. From then on when I arrive for my appointments, I bring several books, magazines, and schoolwork.

The atmosphere in his waiting room is always one of comraderie and hope. Dr. Zimbler and I are on a mission together.

I find a healer with a heart.

THE FOG

The task which her own mother may have failed to perform, she must perform.

Marion Woodman

I am trapped in a white fog, a swirling mist of echoing beeps. Eyes shut.

"Are you awake? Peggy, Peggy, it's all done. We called your brother and he knows. He's coming to see you later. "

"Uh huh. Is there a ship on my leg? It's so heavy and it's killing me."

"A ship on your leg? I'll give you more medicine for the pain. There's no ship. Take deep breaths through the mask."

"What time is it?"

"It is 6 o'clock."

The surgery started at 10.

The whole day is gone. I can't move. I don't want to move. I want to go home. I made a terrible mistake. It is too late now. Now I've done it.

Nurses swarm around me. I am freezing. The monitors beep.

"Dr. Zimbler wants an x-ray."

Now?

His voice is behind me. A massive machine looms over me. A plate slides under the cast.

No, no, don't touch me.

The x-ray is done. Dr. Zimbler likes how it looks.

I hurt. I'm scared I'll lie like this forever.

The surgical nurse asks, "Are you okay?"

I am not okay. I am trained to say, I am okay. I am not okay. This pain will kill me. I cannot live like this. This was a huge mistake. Now I know.

From the waist down my body is on fire.

Dr. Zimbler warned me about discomfort. He didn't say agony. Why isn't the pain medication working?

Male orderlies roll my bed towards an elevator. They speak gently. I moan. The elevator is huge. It looks like a freight elevator. I am surrounded. I look around. I close my eyes.

Where are we? Don't let the bed bump.

It bumps going over the lip of the elevator. I feel it.

Don't touch me.

Rows of lights shine above me. We are not in the recovery room anymore. We're in the hall of the orthopedic floor. The doors swing open. The lights are too bright. Someone is yelling, "Help me, please." They sound desperate. The nurse says the yeller just had her hip replaced.

I'm in my room on 3W. I'm rolled next to a window.

The nurse in my room asks, "How are you?"

"Fine."

I am not fine. I am not fine. I don't know what all this equipment is.

"It is done for today," a nurse says. Your left foot is done.

A technician comes to set up traction. He is quiet. I am glad.

Don't talk to me.

There are weights clanging on the side of the bed.

Be careful. Don't touch me.

"I'll need to lift up your leg for a moment."

Be careful, okay?

The leg is wrapped in a soft cast up to my thigh. The cast is far away from my eyes.

Does my foot look straight? David will know. I have to remember to ask. I am so scared.

I hope I can do this. I can do this. I am not sure I can do this.

David is looking at me. He has a suit on. I try not to cry.

Is my foot straight? Is it at a 90-degree angle?

He says it is.

Are you sure? Then it's worth it.

I am flat on my back with no way out. Someone comes in and puts an IV in my right top wrist. It is for fluids, she says. She tapes the tube down.

There is too much stuff on me.

David keeps looking at me. "Are you okay? Are you sure? I will be back tomorrow. We are worried about you. It took eight hours."

"That is really long. Tell Linda I am okay."

I am not okay. I am sure I am not okay. She will want to know that I am.

David is gone.

I hope he comes back.

Dr. Zimbler comes in and asks how I am doing. I say fine.

I am not fine. I am nauseous. What if I throw up? My body feels heavy and useless. It's still so foggy.

Nurses come in and out and adjust the bed, the pillows, and the rail.

The blood pressure cuff feels too tight.

Machines beep. The nurses are very calm and move fast. Dr. Zimbler says he did everything he wanted with the left foot and leg. He still has his green scrubs on. The right foot surgery is Monday.

There's blood on his scrubs. My blood. He looks so different in scrubs. He has muscles and green slippers on his shoes. He pats my arm. He says I did well. I think that means he is proud of me for not losing too much blood. I feel like the good student. He will come back tomorrow.

I hope he does. I feel safe with him in the room.

The soft cast is just temporary to let the leg swell.

"Okay. Thank you so much." *What have I done? What if I never stand again?*

The room is dark for a few minutes. The tv is off. There is a window to my right. Someone is at the foot of my bed. I squint to see who it is.

It was Jean. She used to be a good friend of mine. She had an uncorrected cleft palate. Her speech was distinctive. That's how I knew it was Jean. She was a Christian Science practitioner. She prayed for our family. She and I used to have an appointment every Saturday. I talked to her about my mom's cancer. She tried to help me not be scared. But I was scared. I was very scared. We talked about God and healing. But Mom died.

We're not such good friends lately. I disappointed her when I said I was going to have surgery. I told her it's not too late for her either. She didn't like that. So I walked out of her office. She cried. I am not sure why.

"Peggy, Peggy."

"Yah? It really hurts. It really hurts."

She tells me that's because I have turned away from God. Turned away and didn't trust. "Get out of my room and don't come again." I'm shocked I can talk that loud.

Jean walks out.

Who invited her to come? What does she know?

She knows a lot. She knows what it is like to be different. She knows what it is like to be stared at the minute she talks.

How does she have faith to go on? Well, I don't.

I can't believe I did this. I hope I haven't made a big mistake.

Someone comes in and wants me to blow in a tube. I can hardly do it. It tastes funny. She tells me to try again. She doesn't want me to get pneumonia from the anesthesia. I blow some more. She says she will be back tomorrow to do it again.

Everybody is coming back tomorrow.

A nurse tries to spoon red jello into my mouth. I don't want it. She says I need to swallow so I can pee.

There is too much to do. I just want to moan all by myself. No jello.

It is almost time for my morphine I hope.

The nurse lifts up the sheet and injects me in my bottom. I don't care if it hurts.

It doesn't work enough. I thought painkillers kill pain. They don't.

Linda pokes her head in. She asks how I am.

"Fine."

I am not fine.

She sits on a chair across from me. David is home with the kids. She does not say anything about God. That is nice of her.

A nurse wants me to try to pee again. It's hard not to cry.

I cannot pee on command.

The nurse turns on the water in the little sink to see if it will help. It does not. It is important she says.

I would if I could.

If I can't, I will need to be catheterized.

That does not sound fun.

But I can't pee. Linda leaves. She will be back another day.

"Okay. Thanks for everything." The words come out slowly.

She is so lucky she can go home.

Finally I can close my eyes. The nurse keeps checking my vitals. I learn what vitals are. Another nurse adds a second IV to make sure there is no infection. Now I have two in one arm. *I cannot get comfortable. I feel the cold liquid going up my vein. Is this normal? I can't change positions. I hurt too much to sleep.*

The nurse asks me to pee on the bedpan. Still no go. She leaves it on the side table. She sends for a nurse to catheterize me.

I don't care, just do it.

A male nurse comes in.

I don't care that he's a male.

He is so gentle and it's done fast.

I don't need to worry about that anymore.

I have tubes going in and out of me. Every function is monitored. Numbers flash on screens.

Returning to Combat

I can't believe it's Monday, even though the days have crawled by. I spend the days writhing in my bed, sipping cranberry juice, and waiting for David to visit each night. I still count the hours until my next morphine shot. I mark five days by the nurses' changing shifts. At night they take my temp and blood pressure every two hours by flashlight. The nurse scolds, "Are you still awake?" The night nurse is a taskmaster. No sleeping pills after 3 am.

The lights are on in the hall. Buzzers go off all night. Patients cry out. Are they in pain or having nightmares?

I'd give anything for a hot shower or to have my hair washed.

I can't imagine having surgery again today. But I need matching feet. That is the whole point of correcting both feet in one hospitalization. Hopefully, I'll only be out of school for five months. If I did one foot and then waited a year or so, to do the other, I'd miss another five months. I have plenty of sick days. That's not the point. But it was in the days when I thought I was irreplaceable as a teacher. It's totally unthinkable to need to be absent like this twice. That was my naïve logic.

Surgery is at 11 am. They're going to change the cast on my left leg and foot during the surgery for the right foot. I'm relieved I won't see my feet and legs with stitches and staples yet. That won't happen until next week. A nurse promises to give me a pill to calm me down before surgery. I could use one immediately. I have stomach cramps already.

I use the bedpan and see that I have my period. No wonder my stomach hurts. I ask for a Tampax. The nurse says they are not allowed but brings a big pad. Since underwear is not worn, I ask how it will stay in place.

She says, "Put it over the right spot and don't worry about it."

The nurse is not rude and isn't worried about it. Some people are more relaxed than others. I'm not one of them.

I click on the tv overhead. I haven't watched the news for five days. A nurse is in the room capping off my IVs for surgery. My veins are black and blue and tender as if I've been in combat.

The newscaster reports that a Christian Science couple is being prosecuted for the death of their son, Roy. He had a bowel obstruction and his parents did not take him to the hospital or doctor. They relied on God for healing. A church spokesman makes a statement. He tries to defend what happened by saying medical care is not foolproof either. I know about this case from the news already. I wonder why he can't just say this is a tragedy and it shouldn't ever happen, especially to a child.

The nurse stops to watch the report and comments, "How can parents do that? It is so irresponsible."

I pretend I'm an innocent bystander. I'm an undercover spy, experiencing a different way to get help.

An intern appears at the foot of my bed and explains the schedule again. Anxiety meds at 10.

I need them right now. But I'm not used to demanding anything. After the meds, I'll transfer to a gurney. No traction while moving to the same operating room like last Thursday. Dr. Zimbler will meet me there. I can't believe I'm doing this again.

I spend the remaining hours with my eyes closed. I'm not feeling brave. I sing hymns to myself over and over. Tears come. Jean said I deserted God. Why is there a chapel in hospitals if God deserts the patients? I think God is with me. I haven't totally lost her faith.

My stepmother calls to wish me well. My father gets on the phone and sounds like he wants *me* to comfort him. He spouts spiritual absolutes. I feel more anxious than before the call. I wish my mom were alive. She'd be patting and holding my hand. My mom was a tender comforter. She'd loyally come and sit with me in a hospital or anywhere. Mom would say, "Want me to sing 'O Gentle Presence' to you?"

Suddenly I'm freezing cold and feel sick to my stomach. If I were at home, I'd sit on the toilet.

The orderlies bring in a gurney covered in flannel sheets. They undo the traction contraption.

I hope the anxiety meds will kick in soon.

I imagine it will feel better not to be tethered up, but I'm so wrong. They lower my leg down on the bed. It's excruciating. They tell me to slide over to the gurney. It looks too narrow. I'm certain I cannot do it. Every tiny movement of my body shoots searing pain into my leg and foot.

The orderlies keep apologizing, "We're so sorry. Almost done," as I moan.

I'm finally lying on the gurney. My back throbs lying flat. I'm scared I'll never see this room again. It has become my hospital home. Not that I feel at home, but at least I know all the movements of the shadows, the sounds of the hall, where the phone is.

They roll me into the elevator they used four days ago. I'm pushed towards a staging area hallway for surgery. The gurney is against the wall. The doors automatically open and close. Surgeons go in and out. They are dressed in green scrubs and have masks over their faces. There are so many signs everywhere. Keep out. No smoking. Operating rooms 1-4. The hall is like an underground town.

An orderly stands guard next to me. He's silent. I try to pray. I'm still freezing, even covered with a flannel sheet. I still have stabbing stomach pains.

I tell the orderly. He says just to breathe and relax. He is kind, not impatient. It's impossible to relax with the cast on my throbbing left leg up to her thigh and a pad on.

It's not his fault.

The calming meds start to work and my surroundings start to fade in and out. Voices echo. I'm suddenly afraid I'm going to have diarrhea. I quickly tell the orderly keeping watch but don't use the word *diarrhea*. It's too embarrassing and personal.

Suddenly, my stomach explodes. The diarrhea is unstoppable.

I hear a voice over an intercom say, "Dr. Zimbler, we need some time."

I'm half-drugged but totally mortified. "I'm sorry, I'm so sorry." A nurse appears and leans over me. "Don't you worry."

I don't remember being cleaned up. I can't believe strangers had to do that. Later a friend says, "Oh they're used to everything." No one at the hospital ever mentions it, but I'm still embarrassed 31 years later when the image again pops into my head.

PART IV

THE WARRIOR

SCAFFOLDING

...Nothing has been wasted; for the soul doesn't waste anything.
Michael J. Meade

The words *inner scaffolding* came as an image one night. A perfect metaphor for me. A gift from nightly musings and meditations.

I needed new physical scaffolding, which I received with my surgery. I visually saw the scaffolding holding up my body. The different medical procedures and doctors created that.

But the inner scaffolding work was mine to do. It had to be built from scratch. My inner scaffolding continually said I had fallen short of spiritual expectations. I'd disappointed my family, Christian Science friends, and church, just to get a new outer scaffolding: straight feet.

The old inner scaffolding voices needed replacing. But more importantly I needed to have a new scaffolding to replace them. Stronger, healthier scaffolding, which demanded I use my new, more informed voice. The voice that reported that choices exist and are allowable. The old scaffolding of self-hate, guilt, inferiority, and sorrow began to have less power.

Now that my outer scaffolding became steady, I needed to rearrange and replace my inner scaffolding to reflect the new information my psyche presented. I imagined climbing up that scaffolding on the rungs of courage, self-worth, confidence, and validation. Authentic writing helped. Words became less daunting, knowing that my words can be changed, refined, believed. My new inner scaffolding, a surging story that needed to be told.

It is the essence of who I am.

This metaphor helped me feel closer to my mother even in her death. I felt watching her pain was pointless and separated us forever. Now I see that her dying, strangely enough, gave me an even deeper connection to her. Courage, a rung of my inner scaffolding was a gift directly from her. Mom transferred the courage she used to endure unending pain, to me, so that I didn't need to be burdened by pain for the rest of my life.

BONES AND SOUL

You're coming with me, poor thing, you don't know how to speak. You don't know how to sing. I will teach you.

Joy Harjo

Once I began thinking about my life as having both physical and psychological scaffolding, the surgery takes on even greater meaning. Saying yes to the procedure broke with my beliefs and upbringing. I had planned to rely on spiritual healing for the rest of my life. My past crumbled with the reorganization of my bones, tendons, muscles, and ligaments by a doctor. That was the outward destruction of old thoughts and past decisions. It was the building of trust that perhaps, there is more than one answer. Perhaps, a humble human can also be a healer.

I'd imagined that after my body healed, I'd go back to my old life and religion. Instead, the surgery caused internal action and reorganization as well as physical change. I tried to go back but felt too uncomfortable and upset. I was shunned by some and felt alienated by others. I didn't belong to the church anymore.

At first, I experienced a tidal wave of sadness and fear. I struggled to "get back to normal." But no normal sat there waiting for me. Just like in art, I started over with a blank canvas.

I searched for consistency in my own voice, not the voice of the church. What would that new voice say? For a while there was no new voice, just my old voice. It condemned me. It told me I had fallen from the standard. My old voice was the church's voice.

I was excited about my corrected feet, but didn't know who that made me? Now I was trying to figure that out. Who should I listen to?

How does a person get their own voice at this late stage? Choices vs. dogma. My voice vs. hierarchy's voice.

I struggled mentally and emotionally. I needed new internal scaffolding. But what to fill my soul with if not with the formal religion? If not the rules, what?

Maybe I was not a loser. Maybe it made sense to have surgery. Maybe what I'd been believing was misinformation or information I didn't need to live by any longer. I can listen to Mary Baker Eddy, or Carl Jung, or Marion Woodman, or Dr. Zimbler, or anyone I want.

Adjusting to freedom when I had all my answers memorized for so long felt uncomfortable. I was a native in a foreign land.

I worked on cultivating a voice and listening to it. I listened to what made sense for me. My new voice told me I had been controlled or maybe I had become a *dissident*. That dreaded word discussed at dinner so long ago.

But my thinking, reading, social life, health had been controlled. That piece of scaffolding needed discarding. It dawned on me that I'm the kind of person who needs to be able to think and not be told what to do at each step. I need to be able to change my mind. I feared doing that made me a dissident. But my new voice told me it made me free. Creative. When I learn something new, I use that knowledge. It does not have to agree with my former religion. I slowly built my confidence in my truth. I started to understand what was making me feel crazy all along. I was living something that I couldn't really wholeheartedly accept, demonstrate, or feel comfortable with. Not living my truth was destroying my individuality and mental health, not to mention my body.

I needed to feel like a real person, not just an idea. I had split off from my emotions and body to guard myself. I survived depression and angst by staying distanced far from my body. Gradually I moved closer to my body and soul.

I still had large holes to fill. The bones have healed; now the soul must heal and grow strong. My inner voice finally said I'd been brave, not cowardly, to leave the religion. Some might disagree, but that is okay. My voice and decision counted.

I started to accept my creative side again. Not repress it, judge it, and deny it. That helped me be able to verbalize how I'd been living and how it didn't work for me.

I felt I could never qualify as a woman, just an it. I started to see my inner scaffolding of feminine power. Not the clothes, makeup, subservient kind of womanhood. The lion kind, the mother kind, the just kind, the creative kind. All these are feminine qualities that I'd always possessed but hidden.

My journey to new insights has been full of depression and angst. I am learning it is okay to accept the horror and the joy. The shadow and the light. The long journey, not a day trip. I don't need to feel guilty to be happy or alive.

I used to blame my mother for giving me birth. Naively I felt she had caused my clubfeet. I had to blame someone. But there was no blame to be had in reality. Clubfeet, my fate. My destiny, yet to be determined by my exploration of life. Now I envisioned my mother giving me birth and rebirth.

She gave her life for the religion. Because of her I saw that I could no longer do that. She wanted me to live and be free. We are intertwined positively, more than I ever thought. I tried to figure out what she died for. Was it just for a religion, to be faithful?

Did she die to show what can happen if you have no voice? Did she die to show what can happen if you are not open to change?

Death will happen anyway, but a life that you choose suddenly feels important.

To live with self-respect and self-care became her legacy to me. I'll never stop learning or searching for answers and truths that resonate with me. I'll always have many questions. I also have confidence in my new knowledge that *I* believe.

The Unveiling

Straight feet, slender toes, and a heel. When I was little, I'd pull the bed sheets back in the morning. I inspected my feet after praying the night before. Crestfallen, I eventually stopped expecting a morning miracle. I should have thanked those feet for walking with me at all.

When I contemplated surgery, perfection was no longer a goal. I needed feet to walk for the next 40 years. Sturdy ankles that could take the pressure. Fusing joints was fine with me. It takes creativity to build a stable heel. I could live with scars. Lengthen that Achilles tendon any way possible. Get those feet facing forward.

Dr. Zimbler relocated me to a gigantic room after the second surgery. Three or four patients could have fit with ease. But I was the only occupant. He explained he needed space for the people, supplies, and paraphernalia when he changed the casts from soft to hard. He'd have his intern there, a resident, and a nurse to assist. He wanted another nurse to hold my hand for the unveiling.

The entourage entered en masse.

The nurse removed the top bed sheet. An intern and nurse slid blue plastic liners under me. The liners protected the sheet from the wet fiberglass for the casts, and the water and soap needed for disinfecting the sutures. An orderly undid the traction and lowered both legs.

Post-surgery, I was still "uncomfortable." That's what Dr. Zimbler called gut-wrenching pain. But my adrenaline was surging watching this team swoop in and organize. I was pumped to see my feet. I was equally leery of catching a view of the stitches and staples that held them together.

A cart with fiberglass rolls and a huge basin of water stood at the end of my bed. Antiseptic liquid soap, towels, and sponges filled one table. And to my right, scissors in various strange angles waited to cut off the bandages. The orderly rolled in a big trashcan like a custodian uses. I raised the bed with the remote to observe it all. Dr. Zimbler told the hand-holding nurse to get ready.

The intern soaked the first cast with a sponge until it seemed drenched. I felt the warm water seep through the cloth cast and tickle my leg. Then slowly Dr. Zimbler started cutting the layers of bandages off. Five, six, seven, layers. There was special surgical gauze covering the foot and calf. It had a plastic sheen. I turned the other way for a minute but actually didn't want to miss this. Instead I looked with half-closed eyes. Dr. Zimbler explained each step before it happened. Everyone was silent, deferring to his exact instructions. A drum roll would have been perfect.

The nurse removed the blood-covered gauze. The leg and foot were dark orange. They rinsed off the special surgical soap. My nerve endings exploded.

"Breathe," the nurse whispered, patting my head. The swollen foot and brand new heel stared right at me. It looked alien. It was straight, totally straight. There were big black stitches covering the top and side of my ankle. The resident dabbed the stitches vigorously with cotton and some kind of stinging disinfectant.

Dr. Zimbler spoke softly to the intern telling him what to observe. He mentioned swelling, closure, rotation, and angle. He pointed to where the pins were embedded in the foot to hold it all together while it healed.

I didn't yet know they'd have to be removed surgically at a later date.

The resident held my left leg up. I squeezed the nurse's hand hard. Dr. Zimbler held a mirror to the back of the leg for me. There was a row of ugly black staples from the back of my new heel up the length of my calf.

"I feel like I might faint."

"You're okay, deep breaths." The hand-holding nurse leaned in.

I was glad to be lying down. How the hell did he manage to get a normal looking leg and foot out of the mess I came in with?

To me, the new appendage felt like it might float over the top of the bed into the heavens. It had no gravity of its own. I was disconnected from it, except for the pain.

The intern dried the foot and leg thoroughly with a terry cloth towel. The friction felt like rubbing nails into my skin. I sucked the air in through my teeth.

"Take a minute to regroup," Dr. Zimbler encouraged.

Meanwhile fiberglass rolls soaked in warm water. The hand-holding nurse stood by for phase two. The resident held up the bare leg again. Dr. Zimbler placed soft cotton stocking from the foot to the knee. He cut the tip off so all toes showed. He'd need to check and make sure circulation was always flowing. Then he started rolling the fiberglass around the foot forming a cast. There was a slapping sound as he stretched the material around my foot in a figure 8 configuration. The fiberglass heated up as he worked. I had no idea that was going to happen. Dr. Zimbler firmly squeezed the material so it formed exactly to the foot and leg. The pressure was more than intense. His gloved hands felt like a vice. He made sure the angle was correct, pushing and holding the ankle to a perfect 90 degrees. Moaning and groaning would have helped. But I was afraid it would sound ungrateful.

I took deep breaths trying to focus on how exciting this really was. There should have been a brass band playing to mark this victorious event. The artistry, technical difficulty, and devotion to detail made my heart ache. I felt the strangest mix of elation, pain, fear, and nausea.

Dr. Zimbler lay the "finished" leg down on a pillow. He proclaimed, "The healing is going well." No infection and all the incisions were knitting together. The intern and nurse cleaned up the mess to start on the right foot! Two beautiful casts later, my legs were back in traction. The orderly swooped in and threw out all the blue coverings.

That morning was a tiny turning point. I finally saw with my own eyes why there was so much grinding pain. I eyed each incision and every suture. Now I knew what was going on under those casts. The next day Percocet became my painkiller. No more Morphine. Pills instead of injections. Progress.

As Dr. Zimbler and his group headed towards the door that day, he nonchalantly said, "So that's how this works. We'll do it again next week." He looked serious. This was no joke.

"What? Next week, again?" I couldn't believe this was going to become a routine.

Dr. Zimbler was a master at not getting ahead of the process. "Yes," he said matter-of-factly. "As the swelling goes down, the casts will become too large and will get very uncomfortable. We need to keep changing them weekly to keep them snug. And we always check for infection. You'll get used to this."

And with that, the entourage left my room to tend to more miracles, like it was nothing.

My first response to seeing my new feet and legs was shock. My body responded by feeling freezing cold. It was hard to decipher specific thoughts at that moment. In hindsight I was witnessing a miracle. I had prayed for decades to God, but my answer was from a human. Perhaps Dr. Zimbler had divine talent, a surgical gift.

The feeling of my legs not being attached and flying overhead to the heavens, Well perhaps they wanted to show my mom. Here they are! What we both longed for. It's happened.

Gratitude and grief were strong as the recasting process began. Light and dark. I held both of them and still do.

I had gratitude for this father figure at the foot of my bed who listened to what I needed. A listening, loving voice that I hadn't had with my own father. Gratitude that Dr. Z. took my case. Gratitude that he had the maturity, expertise, compassion, and artistry to rebuild my feet that defined my life.

OVER THE EDGE

What needs to be counted to have a voice? Courage. Anger. Love.
Something to say; Someone to speak to; Someone to listen.
Terry Tempest Williams

9:30 am, Monday through Friday, the physical therapist stood at my bedside at Newton-Wellesley Hospital. A coach with no whistle. She'd already taught me to sit up, grabbing the hanging triangle over my bed with both hands. "No more using the remote control," she commanded.

Today's agenda? Easing my casts over the side of the bed.

I had imagined that after surgery, I would be upright within weeks and walking without any intermediary steps. Now I understood that a rigid protocol existed. Every new motion had to be done incrementally to avoid an accident or injury.

I grabbed the hanging traction triangle with both hands and sat straight up. I asked for a second hospital gown, trying to procrastinate. One was on backwards already, and this one I put on like a robe. I needed to cover my backside for this new move.

It would take more than that to make me feel less helpless. Trusting a PT that she wouldn't let me break my neck. Trusting the doctor that he really would get me out of this hospital. Trusting myself that I was not in over my head. Trust for me defied my neurotic nature of predicting the worst.

Today, the PT's goal to help me towards regaining independence was to introduce my new feet to the world of movement.

My world was my hospital bed, where I was still encased in medical equipment. Dr. Zimbler assured me I'd walk again but just not yet. I was in a "relearning mode," he encouraged. Relearning how to sit, to dangle my feet, transfer to the wheelchair, and eventually bear my weight.

Today, I was ready for feet dangling.

The PT had retaught me to bend my knees the week before. I was shocked how painful it was moving my sore joints after two weeks in straight-legged traction. When I mentioned this to her, she told me how much harder it is having this surgery as an adult.

This I knew.

The PT unclipped the traction. She gently laid each casted leg flat onto the bed. I reminded myself these appendages belonged to me. It was up to me to see what they could do. She guided me as I slowly rotated my upper body, then my legs. Finally I sat sideways on the bed.

"Breathe, please." Each new movement made me hold my breath. She asked that I inch my way to the edge and ease my legs down off the side of the bed.

She warned me that I'd probably feel a rush of sensation. No blood had circulated from my knees down since before surgery, to avoid swelling.

The minute my casted legs went over the side of the bed, they seemed to each weigh 40 pounds. I could feel the rush of blood back to my feet. Enormous pressure engorged each foot. Perhaps my feet and legs didn't fit in the casts anymore. They raged to get out. Ready to burst.

I imagined my upper body plummeting to the linoleum floor with my legs acting as anchors.

"Okay, that's enough, that's enough." I begged. "Let's try it for two minutes." She took out her stopwatch.

"This is really too much." How awful was this going to be?

"The more you do it, the easier it will become."

I recognized this kind of pep talk. I had used this strategy on my elementary students, encouraging them as they learned to read.

I looked up at the ceiling lights, squinted and moaned. My head throbbed. The sweat ran down my cleavage.

Finally the PT helped me ease my legs back onto the bed and she reattached my traction.

I felt like I had been running laps in gym. Out of breath and sweaty. "I didn't know this would be so hard." I caught my breath as my limp body shuddered.

"Tomorrow we'll do four minutes. In no time we will have you in a wheel chair." I should have been elated at the prospect of being in a wheelchair. But how would I learn to get back into bed by myself? And how would I ever learn to transfer to a toilet?

"How will I ever walk again if putting my feet over the edge is this hard?"

"Well, it will happen. I promise." And out she went to her hip replacement patient.

I sat in bed stunned by the work ahead. I had originally thought the operation was the worst challenge I'd face. Now each new phase seemed out of my reach. I pressured myself to be competent immediately. I never wanted to embarrass myself and look weak, not just here in the hospital. I recognized this trend of mine.

Slow down, said an invisible voice.

Each morning we upped the dangling time. By the end of the week I sat with my legs over the edge of the bed for 10 minutes. When I told visitors about this feat, they were not that impressed. The fast-paced outside world was so different from my slow-motion hospital days.

In my orthopedic world, a ten-minute victory was plenty for me to mull over until bedtime. I was not interested in watching tv.

My own drama held my attention 24/7.

The next Monday the PT rolled in a wheelchair.

I held my breath.

This time she had me back up to the edge of the bed. Then she guided me how to "transfer" with my legs still on the bed. I used my arm strength to hold onto the railings of the locked wheelchair and to lift my bottom into the chair. Then we raised the legs of the chair up horizontally and carefully placed the casts in each pillowed leg holder.

Voilà, I'd gone from a floppy mop of a body to Wonder Woman.

But at night my euphoria vanished. The dark erased any confidence. I wondered if I'd ever be able to teach again. To focus on something other than my legs, my feet, my balance, my pain.

When would I be discharged to my brother's house? Could I get up the stairs in my own condo? Could my re-formed left foot learn to use the clutch on my Honda? Worries came rushing in between midnight and 3 am.

I had time. It was early May, although not April anymore.

As I said, I was scheduled to go back to teaching full time in September. At this stage in my career I thought my new first graders needed ME. NO substitute would do. Only I could introduce them to the wonders of reading.

When I had asked my school system for a medical leave, five months seemed like plenty of time. How optimistic. I was used to not limiting myself. In the past, that meant pushing myself much further than I could really take. Like going to school with the flu, or only taking two days off when my mom died. Now, seeing the effort it took to sit in a wheelchair, I couldn't imagine being discharged from the hospital, never mind teaching full time.

What would I do when 20 first-graders came in to my classroom, energized for the day?

THE EMBOLISM

The tenth day of my hospitalization, May first, was a Saturday. The next week held a projected discharge to my brother's home. I'd be recuperating where spiritual healing was practiced with a family who was "absent from the body, and present with the Lord." Hopefully I'd be back to my own home by the end of July, walking. I couldn't quite imagine.

So far both feet had been corrected. I was off morphine but not weight-bearing yet. Imbedded surgical pins still held all ten toes straight and my fused ankles in place. The stitches and staples hadn't been removed. The hospital had scheduled a June 8th surgery to remove the pins. My casts, below the knees at last, allowed for bending. Three days before the projected discharge, the weekend nurse came in with her clipboard ready for business. I recognized her. She was the nurse who had worked with me for three days to get off morphine. I went from morphine every six hours to twice a day to once a day… and bingo, just Percocet.

What now? She had that look. Here comes a new mission.

Narcotic medicine caused constipation, she reminded me. The nurse gave me a stern pep talk about why bowel movements were important. "Uh huh," I replied, trying to sound interested. Seriously, this was the least of my problems. She asked me if I was swallowing my pink milk of magnesia every night. I confessed no.

"You'll have to have an enema if you don't have one by tonight," she threatened.

I'd heard of those. I promised I'd try.

Around noon I was able to have a bowel movement. I won't go into the pain or the relief I felt at conquering this feat. No enema for me. The nurse seemed less like an army sergeant after that. She gave me a smile and a nod. She'd completed her mission.

An hour later, I couldn't catch my breath. I changed my position in the hospital bed. There weren't many ways to move with my legs still in traction. Perhaps I had gotten myself upset by the bowel movement. I always blamed myself for any strange anxiety or pain. I recited a hymn in my head, "In atmosphere of love divine, I live and move and breathe. Though mortal eyes may see it not, tis sense that would deceive." Hymns had acted as my Valium for 37 years. Having been taught that my body lied, I learned to deny and ignore aches and pains.

Should I tell someone? Or should I deny my breathlessness? These two conflicting thoughts were like a tennis match. Back and forth, back and forth. The ball was my thinking. One player was a Christian Scientist, the other someone relying on medicine. I wasn't sure which player I was. I still could not catch my breath. I hated to bother the nurses, but finally decided I'd better tell someone.

I pushed my little buzzer. The sergeant nurse came in. I questioned, "Is it normal not to be able to catch my breath?" She took one look at me and called for some kind of cart.

Suddenly all kinds of doctors appeared. Instantly I had an oxygen mask strapped to my mouth and nose. Someone was taking my blood pressure. Orderlies quickly transferred me to a gurney and raced down the hall to another floor.

I hadn't expected such a commotion. Frightened and shocked, I started praying. My body was too demanding lately. *See what happens when you turn away from God and start listening to your body?* My guilt responses, still firmly intact.

A nurse stayed with me as I lay on a gurney in the hall. I was taken inside a darkened room for some kind of scan. The scan doctor asked me when the shortness of breath first began. I was embarrassed to tell him that it was after the bowel movement. I really can't name the scan or recall all the details of this emergency because my feet were killing me from lying flat and not in traction. The toddler PTSD from a mask covering my face came rushing right back in. I shook like an entrapped animal but didn't dare rip the oxygen mask off.

The doctor scanned my lungs. I guess you could say I entered the underworld. This was the bleakest event of my hospital stay. Maybe I was right there in the labyrinth in front of the Minotaur. I definitely could not slay that Minotaur alone, but my voice had set off a chain of heroes who could. The doctors and medicine came to my rescue. My golden thread out of danger.

When I returned to my room, a new IV pole waited for me. An IV nurse inserted a big fat needle into my already black-and-blue arm. As she hooked me up to Heparin, a blood thinner, the night nurse explained that I had had an embolism. She suggested it was probably from lying in bed for 10 days. I had never heard of an embolism or Heparin.

Dr. Zimbler appeared with an entourage of other doctors. Called at home by the hospital, he raced over all dressed up on the way to a family wedding. He greeted me with "The surgery was a success but we almost lost the patient." His concern made me nervous. He explained that most probably a clot had formed in one leg and moved up to my lung. I'd need to be on a blood thinner for the next nine months. I'd have the IV for at least a week in the hospital. Then I'd go on a pill called Coumadin after my release. He said it was very good I HAD told the nurse. I could imagine the talk by my fellow church members if I had not told the nurse and died. *Too bad she turned away from the Truth to medicine. What a shame.*

Dr. Zimbler admonished me: "Whenever you feel anything off or odd, immediately tell the nurse. Always." I felt tears spring into my eyes. Here I was with an IV again after just getting rid of the one that fights infections. My hospital stay was being extended.

"I will see you on Monday, dear." Dr. Zimbler left.

I felt strangely loved. My mom used to call me "dear."

By then I was certain I had done the right thing to report my breathlessness. Perhaps it helped that the day before a Christian Science practitioner startled me awake from a nap.

It wasn't Jean, who had told me I deserved to be in pain after abandoning my beliefs after the first surgery. It was Betty who smiled at me in my hospital bed. I'd known her since I was a toddler. She had been a friend of my mom's. She was less intense than other practitioners my parents had dragged me to in search of spiritual healing.

She had driven all the way from New Hampshire to look in on me. The minute I saw her, I began to cry. I told her I felt so guilty for choosing the medical path. In our religion it was either the physical path or the metaphysical path. No mixing methods allowed. One counteracted the other. I knew what I was expected to follow, but I hadn't. I told her about Jean telling me I had abandoned my belief in God. She shook her head and assured me I had absolutely been so "faithful." Although she used the religious lingo like "faithful, path, obedience," etc., she was trying to reassure me that God was still with me and I could not be separated from his love.

I asked, "Even in the hospital?"

She replied, "Especially in the hospital."

Betty was a free spirit and thinker, and I appreciated her vote of confidence.

She didn't stay long but held my hand and told me to stop "fretting" and rest. I went on crying. I was not used to compassionate responses from my "religious people."

None of my other Christian Science friends visited me in the hospital. Even my father stayed clear of the place. Hospitals scared them, I hypothesized. I knew they did me. Foreign territory. A last resort, risky business. I'll always be grateful to my brother, who visited every single day. He visited every night at 6:00. I could count on it.

After a week on Heparin, I took my first ride in an ambulance to David's house. Finally discharged after 17 days. My arrival made quite the scene as the neighborhood children surrounded the ambulance in my brother's driveway.

I immediately handed David my prescription for Percocet. I needed another pill in an hour. He loyally hustled to his car and drove off to the local pharmacy to fill his first-ever prescription.

A "blood man" named Vern arrived each morning to make sure my blood was thin enough. He'd call the results in to Dr. Zimbler. I looked out the window from my twin bed at the crack of dawn. My room was at the top of the stairs in the split-level house. Linda left the door unlocked so Vern could tiptoe in and not wake up Matthew, and his one year old twin brothers, Chris and Tim.

Seeing Vern's old Toyota Corolla, headlights on, pull into the driveway assured me I'd have at least one visitor that day. Vern was always very cheery, even at 6 am. He took the time to chat, not just draw blood and run. He was a large man, and his gentle presence filled my tiny bedroom. It was a new sensation to continually feel like I was being cared for, not just prayed about. I loved how the vials clanked around in his little carrier as he walked back down the stairs to his car.

I was beginning to get used to seeing my blood fill up glass vials. I'd learned in Sunday school that "man is not made of brain, blood, bones and other material elements." But watching my blood rush into the vial, I saw that I was more than a spiritual idea. I existed as a human. It may sound like an obvious observation, but I used to look in the mirror and wonder if I was a real person or even alive. Gnawing questions. Only decades later did I learn that questioning my existence was a form of depression.

Because I was recuperating 60 miles away from home, my friends from school could only visit on weekends. When my teacher friends entered my room, I was back in my own comfortable world for an hour or two. They caught me up on teacher's room gossip. They brought letters and pictures filled with hearts and flowers from my students in their sweet first-grade handwriting.

Being entertained, the pain subsided. When I finally could leave the house in a wheelchair, they drove me to Bubbling Brook ice cream. We sat in the car and ate black raspberry in a cup. It looked so bright and springy outside. Being out in society was a lift. But seeing how mobile everyone was served as a reality check. I stared at all the moving around that everyone was doing in the parking lot. It looked so easy yet it was certainly out of my reach. I was still in a painkiller fog. I had miles to go before rejoining the living.

Exhaustion hit after the 40-minute outing, and I hadn't even walked. I'd told my principal in April that I'd be back teaching in September. I suddenly realized I might have miscalculated the time I'd need before teaching again.

MY BODY'S VOICE

My blood was drawn, my half of a bagel eaten.

I let my sister-in-law, Linda, know I'd be happy to fold laundry from my bed whenever the dryer beeped. She told me she loved having me recuperate at their house. I was company for her during the 12 hours my brother spent at work.

I never felt like good company.

I banged into the hall walls in my wheelchair on the way to the bathroom. I still needed meals delivered from their kitchen to my room upstairs. I became weepy around 4 pm when the pain peaked again before the 6 pm pill time. Who needs a weepy 38-year-old when there are three children under 4 in the house?

I could entertain Matthew for Linda, when he was willing to lie in my bed calmly to hear a story. But any hint of kicking or roughhousing sent me into a panic, just waiting for a jab to one of my casts. Then the painful reverberation travelled directly to my brain. The twins sat together in my wheelchair staring at me. Who was this person who never went home?

One morning while Linda was delivering my three nephews to pre-school, I felt a peculiar sensation inside my left cast. I felt a tingling, rubbing sensation near the brand new heel. It felt like sand was digging into the skin. I switched concentration to my right cast and foot. No strange feeling there. But my fear antennae went up.

I tried to concentrate on something else. I looked out the window at the quiet neighborhood. Maybe I was being paranoid. Too much lying around thinking about how my body felt. A freezing anxiety crept up my throat. TROUBLE.

I had been used to denying how my body felt for so long. I was losing my knack. I didn't want to become one of those people that complained about every twitch. "Stoic" had been my middle name.

I focused on looking outside, trying to ignore my body for at least a few minutes. No children rode bikes or skateboarded yet in the quiet neighborhood. I waited for Linda's van, anticipating its appearance any moment.

Then I thought back to my embolism, now almost a month before. I remembered what Dr. Zimbler had said to me as he left my room that day. "Always tell the nurse if you feel something strange. Always!" I had not just imagined that embolism.

I had made progress in listening to my body lately. I didn't yet think I was worthy of it particularly; instead, I was just trying to be obedient. I'd been excellent at obedience in my religion. Denying pain was second nature. Patriarchy ruled supreme. Now I had to learn to switch allegiances and be obedient to a new "voice." Maybe this grinding sand sensation was worth reporting.

I dialed Dr. Zimbler's office. I was a familiar patient by then, being the only adult in his pediatric practice. When I reached Susan, the receptionist I reported, "I feel something strange going on under my left cast. It feels sandy and like it is rubbing against my new heel."

Susan transferred me right away to Dr. Zimbler's right-hand man, Bob. Bob was the senior technician, the person who removed and made new casts for Dr. Z. He was so in synch with Dr. Z. that few words were spoken between them. Dr. Z. trusted Bob's handiwork He knew just how much pressure to apply. He made the new casts as comfortable as casts could be. He did all this while exuding confidence, calm, and empathy. Each Saturday Bob carried me gently from my wheelchair up the three steps into Dr. Zimbler's office for recasting. I almost had a crush on him.

Bob told me that I should come right over. He said Dr. Z. was just getting out of surgery in Boston and would meet me at the Newton office. I called my brother at his work number. He was able to drive the 20 minutes home to get me right away. How lucky that David was an executive and could leave like that.

Linda came home in the meantime, but she'd need to stick around to pick the boys back up in two hours. David lifted me down the stairs and into the car. He loaded the wheelchair. He didn't question going to the office yet again.

Bob had the cast saw ready and immediately took both casts off. Dr. Z. inspected the left foot and leg first. "Skin breakdown."

I had never heard that term. He told me it was one of the dangers of surgery on an older patient. That's why they had changed the casts each Saturday, to inspect all areas, as well as refit the casts to the decreased swelling.

Bob took off the right cast off too. Just in case. The right heel was intact.

I asked Dr. Z. what we'd have to do about my left heel?

"We'll clean it up and put you back on antibiotics."

Another setback. I was getting used to them.

Dr. Z. commented, "Luckily it's not down to the bone."

Oh my God, I thought, *let's hope not.*

Dr. Z. praised my calling the minute I felt it. "Breakdown can happen swiftly."

I see the irony now of this observation. I felt like I was always on the verge of "breakdown." Intellectually I knew I had done the right thing by going the medical route. Emotionally I worried, if I could ever come back from it.

Bob put new casts on. On the left cast he cut a window in the heel. The wound was lightly covered with a removable Teflon bandage. He could not give me stitches. The swath of open skin was too wide and deep. He replaced the window with the fitted piece of cutout cast.

The office called a visiting nurse agency and made a daily appointment.

I felt sorry for Dr. Zimbler, who shook his head looking at the deep divot in my new heel. He seemed so bummed that his beautiful artistry was now not as perfect as he had created. Luckily, I could not see the huge gouge in the back of my leg. I was on my back staring at the ceiling tiles. I didn't need any more grossness in my head at that point anyway.

He explained that on June 8th, two weeks away, when they took out the pins in my feet, they'd also do a skin graft from my calf. They'd use that skin on the heel wound. Dr. Z. explained that I'd be under anesthesia during this now double procedure at the hospital. I didn't have any deep fear of a skin graft. At that moment, lying on the table, I was just a too-old clubfoot specimen. Total disaster averted.

And a new "friend" to come calling. Now I had three visitors a day: Vern, my blood man, and Ellen, the visiting nurse, who'd check on the deep divot every day, and apply ointment. Nicole, the PT, stretched my sore casted legs daily getting ready for the grand walk sometime in the near future.

Linda and David never complained about the amount of time I took up. I felt supported. I had the moral support and the medical support I needed. That took some of the pain of the past away.

The breakdown healed easily compared to the rest of my procedures and scars. Now when I look at the back of my left foot, I can see where the stitches lined the graft. The divot looks like a pothole after winter. I see the square of skin on my inner calf where they took the skin for the graft. It has a different texture than the rest of my leg. It never grows hair and I don't need to shave there. My left heel doesn't totally fill out my sneaker, but there is still enough of a heel to hold my foot in.

In my mind I heard my dad telling me that medical procedures are unpredictable and never perfect. My procedure had been human, not divine. A spiritual healing is perfect and leaves "not a trace," he'd pontificate.

That's okay. I do have scars going up my leg and around each foot. But I don't feel totally scarred, like I did all those years searching for my perfect healing.

I was now perfectly cared for by my human healer.

PINS

For some reason the thought of this pin removal hospitalization really threw me. Maybe because by now I understood hospital living and could picture the operating room. I'd need to be hooked up to an IV in the hospital room for Heparin to keep my blood thin the day before the procedure. I wouldn't be in control of my medication, like at home. What if the nurses forgot my pills? What if the pain got so out of control, the meds didn't help? It was hard to be incarcerated after having a brief few weeks of "freedom," and just the thought of getting rolled into an operating room again turned my stomach. On the other hand, I was beginning to feel the pins like interior scaffolding when I tried to curl my toes inside the casts. I didn't want the pins so embedded in my toes, feet, and ankles that I'd need a more complicated surgery.

So I sucked it up and packed just a small backpack for June 8th. I had the urge to pack my own medication. Maybe just for safety, in case the nurses ignored me. So I hid two Percocet in my backpack. I wouldn't be able to reach them anyway. The little closet was at least 5 feet far from my hospital bed. Just security for me, an adult version of a blankie.

An orderly helped me into the hospital bed in the room right across from the nurses' station. It was the room I'd had after my first surgery. Bra off, I put on my little blue johnny.

This time I had a roommate. Her story was worse than mine.

She was a totally normal functioning person working at the upscale Bonwit Teller on Newbury St. in Boston. She was the buyer for women's business clothes. One evening she went to cross the street after work. The sign said walk. As she stepped off the curb, a taxi ran a red light and crashed into her throwing her across the street. She had two broken legs and her pelvis was crushed.

I thought my recuperation loomed large?

By the time she finished her story, she was crying. She told me she was single, with no relatives, and would have to go to rehab at Spaulding Rehabilitation Center in Boston. We bonded immediately. I told her how petrified I was of this next short procedure even though I had two really awful operations just the month before.

She said I had battle fatigue. She made me laugh.

She said when I was done with this procedure, we should order pizza and have it delivered to the room. I didn't know if that was possible, but she said it was. Friends of hers from the clothing store had done that the day before for her. I had something to look forward to.

The orderlies came for me at 10:00 the next morning. As I cried transferring onto the gurney, my roommate said, "I will be right here waiting for you." That made me cry more and then laugh. Where would she go?

"Okay, it's a deal!" I said, as they pushed me out the door. And down I went in the elevator once again to the surgical center. The only thing I remember was that as they rolled me in, the doctors started talking about what the procedure entailed. I heard the utensils clinking on a side table. Then Dr. Zimbler walked in.

I remember telling him urgently I didn't want to hear what they were going to do or see the instruments. I had said that for my first two surgeries and they always gave me a sedative before rolling in. I guess they thought this procedure was peanuts compared to totally remaking each foot and leg.

Quickly Dr. Z. instructed the anesthesiologist to give me "something."

When I woke after the surgery, I was surprised that I was in no more pain than before. I had new casts. My skin graft was completed.

When I rolled back into my room, my roommate clapped. What a treat to wake up and not be in traction and only one IV.

The PT visited me that evening and showed me blue canvas coverings that we'd be putting on the casts, so I could stand up. I thought they looked like clown shoes, but they were mine for the foreseeable future.

Now that the pins were out, weight bearing came next.

My roommate heard the PT tell me the news. "Great news" she called through the curtain dividing our beds. She was my live-in cheerleader.

"I guess," I said. "I don't know if I can do it."

Imagining standing kept me up that night. I couldn't imagine actually putting weight on my new feet. I was scared they'd collapse. Maybe I'd hear cracking sounds as they crumpled underneath me.

The next morning right after breakfast the PT came in with my clown shoes. The nurse unhooked my IV. She gave me another johnny to put on like a bathrobe. First she had me put my casts over the edge of the bed. This I could do. She taught me how to put on the clown shoes. They had Velcro so there wouldn't be any huge learning curve to attaching them. The bottoms were rubber for traction.

The PT gave me a little pep talk about just breathing and easing off the bed to the floor.

It seemed like a long way down.

The PT held me under one arm and the nurse the other. It wasn't excruciating as I had imagined, just intense pressure. I had not been upright since April.

The pain was the same level, thanks to the Percocet they'd given me right before this new move. I stood there for a moment knowing that now the work really had begun. My heels were down flat in the casts. No more walking on my tiptoes.

I had corrected clubfeet.

I was really going to walk again, although I couldn't quite imagine anyone ever letting go of me. The PT explained that once I was discharged, my regular PT would have me start learning to walk with crutches. First, I'd have all the stitches and staples taken out of both legs and feet at Dr. Zimbler's next week. I was going home with shiny metal crutches.

The long drawn-out reconstruction process suddenly picked up speed. Clown shoes and crutches. My prizes for this third surgery.

When the PT and nurse got me back in bed, my roommate suggested we call out for that pizza to celebrate. It was amazing how she could put her agony aside and suggest something fun for us to do. She had a takeout menu from the night her friends had ordered a pizza. She read off the tantalizing choices, and then ordered a large hamburger pizza from a local pizzeria. She gave the address as our room at Newton Wellesley Hospital. The nurse on duty said she'd tell the delivery guy to come to our room. I had money in my wallet in the little closet that she took out for me. I think she got a kick out of helping us do something fun on her watch.

Luckily she didn't find the Percocet I had stashed in my sweatpants pocket for emergencies.

I never forgot that roommate. But strangely we never took each other's contact information. It was like we were in an alternative universe where only the present existed. I was still painfully shy. I'd never have asked for her phone number. Too intrusive. Getting that pizza was the one time we weren't begging for pain meds, just paper plates.

The next morning an ambulance company came and took her to Spaulding. She sobbed as she left our room.

White Socks and Cinder Blocks

Up and down the narrow hallway. Walking in my casts, which were covered with blue canvas walking slippers. The green shag carpet and the flowered wallpaper were my runway. I needed to concentrate using the silver crutches as a launch, not leaning posts.

The PT warned that leaning on crutches damaged underarm ligaments. "So you better learn the proper way and stick to it." She wasn't the warmest individual, but I needed a no-nonsense PT for this next phase of mobility training.

The PT spotted me as I lurched my way down the hall towards my brother and sister-in-law's bedroom. Then came the great turn around, hopefully without getting so tangled that I toppled over. All my life I walked head down, as fast as I could, to avoid meeting anyone's eyes. But here I was post-surgery, the focus of the PT's attention, walking down the hall inch by inch. "Stand up straight, eyes forward. The crutches are for balancing, not leaning."

I'd never had great balance, never been agile. Now I needed some serious athletic skills.

"How does it feel?" she called out every few steps.

I couldn't walk and talk at the same time. When I rolled my eyes, she got the point.

I concentrated, lifting each heavy foot just a tad, so the rubber sole wouldn't catch on the shag carpet. At the end of the hall I sat in the wheelchair for a moment, catching my breath. I wanted to whine, "It feels like I'll never walk comfortably," which was kind of ironic since I never had walked comfortably before surgery.

I still imagined my surgery as the ultimate panacea. But could the painful recovery be penance for leaving my faith? In any case, I secretly allowed myself to hope.

I knew I'd have setbacks along the way, but eventually my surgery decision promised change for the better. I held on to that hope. I had no perspective yet, on what was and what wasn't possible with clubfeet surgery at age 37. Some numbing might be permanent, some toes might never move again. There'd be a range of sensations in each foot, but the residual pain should subside. Time would tell, Dr. Zimbler reminded me.

I felt victorious, cautious, terrified, all wrapped into one intense face and furrowed brow.

"Try to practice walking at least three times a day. Make sure the kids aren't around. Make certain your brother or sister-in-law spots you." The PT had many demands.

July was fast approaching. Dr. Zimbler hoped within a week of this initial practice in my casts that I'd be ready for walking casts and new sneakers. The pace had to quicken if I was going to resume teaching in the fall. I had to get my optimism and fortitude revved up.

Linda spotted me when the PT left. She had just watched her twins learn to walk, so she knew all the encouraging phrases. "Good job, nice and slow, you have this. Amazing!"

Another labyrinth journey, though in a straight line down the hall, the Minotaur of doubt staring at me with each step. Linda and I pushed through that blob of fear each time we practiced. I was big on willpower. Linda, in her faith in God, a different kind of warrior.

Saturday at Dr. Zimbler's, new style casts surprised me. Bob crafted the casts as usual but then took his saw and made two vertical cuts so that I had two pieces to each cast.

Bivalve casts. These were officially "walking casts." He took them into another room, lined them with soft cotton, and adhered straps and buckles to the outside of each creation. Now I'd be able to take the casts on and off quickly.

I'd need to buy sneakers and continually practice walking, first with the walking casts, and then switch to the sneakers. The sneakers and casts played complementary roles. Sneakers to practice walking, with a little less rigid support. The casts for added support when my feet got tired or too painful. I'd also sleep in them to keep my straight feet and new heels at a 90-degree angle.

I wanted to cry, "I'm not ready for this." Walking casts, sneakers, too much, too demanding. But then again, the sooner I walked, the sooner I'd be back home in my own condo. Independent again. Driving again.

I kept thinking if I mastered the sneakers, maybe I'd be able to wear flats or Birkenstocks someday. Yet sometimes I just wanted to lie on my back and say, "No, don't make me."

All of a sudden I was trusted with crutches, bivalve casts, and wouldn't I need socks?

Pat, Dr. Zimbler's assistant, came in with a long, rectangular box and pulled out some white nylon socks. Not just any knee socks, *compression* knee socks. They looked very narrow. For good reason. The socks controlled the swelling, as I learned to put consistent pressure on my feet again. Pat told me I'd need to wear these for a year.

Trendy socks, my claim to fame in my school, suddenly took a hit. I always had cool socks to go with my totally uncool shoes. My students loved to see what socks lurked under my cuffs. If we were studying owls, I sported flying owl socks. Planet socks for solar system study. Fish socks the day we visited the New England Aquarium. Magic wands when I read them *Harry Potter.* Myriad pairs. Entertaining first graders, a cinch.

But white socks were a small price to pay for straight feet. Pat rolled one down into a little donut shape and told me to put the top of my foot inside. *Easy for you,* I thought.

My feet felt a bit ethereal and yet often like concrete cinder blocks.

I held my foot gently as I placed it near the sock. The sock rubbed like sand paper when it touched my skin. I'd get used to all these new sensations, Pat said. She had me roll the sock up my leg. The socks felt like moveable vices as they squeezed up to my kneecaps. For the next few days she advised I practice this several times a day and sit with them on for 30 minutes at least.

The squeezing sensation made me queasy.

Dr. Z. came back in and had me put the casts on over the socks to see how that felt. I wound the straps in the figure 8 around each cast.

Dr. Zimbler said, "Hop off the table and try to walk." "Walk with the crutches for a minute so I can make sure they're the right height." He never questioned if I could. Dr. Zimbler, my healer-in chief.

These walking casts felt different from the original casts. In the originals my feet were right against the plaster with gauze bandages. Here in socks, there was a totally different "one step closer to normalcy" sensation.

All the various medical people from his practice peered out their doors. These were the same people who had watched me walk barefoot down the hall before surgery, as I was assessed. Just five months before, they had viewed my x-rays as Dr. Z. discussed complex bilateral clubfeet with them. Now I got the feeling my success was theirs as well, a healing team.

"She's getting sneakers this week," Dr. Z. announced to my smiling audience.

I had this urge to ball my head off, but knew I'd fall flat on my face if I multi-tasked that way.

No one was yelling, *"Walk straight,"* like my grandma used to.

"Go to any sports store and tell them you need high top sneakers, probably men's." Dr. Zimbler acted like it was no big deal. " Don't worry about the size. Get a pair that you can get your foot in without too much pain. Not so large that you trip."

I was used to making a scene at shoe stores just by the deformed feet I always brought in with me. All my life, I'd slinked out of shoe stores as quickly as I could. "Don't look at me," my steely gaze communicated. Now he expected me to announce to some teenage salesboy what I needed, as I took off bivalve casts in a crowded sport's store? Who would drive me to the mall? How would I get into the store itself? What would it feel like to try on myriad pairs of sneakers, when I have been shoeless for months?

Okay, crutches, bivalve casts, compression socks, and sneakers.

Julia, the daughter of the woman who told me after my surgery that I had forsaken God and who lived locally, offered to take me to the mall for the sneaker expedition. I wasn't recuperating in my town, so I couldn't ask school friends to go with me. I hated asking for a ride, but I was far from ready to drive again. Julia and I had known each other since our Sunday school days. I don't know if her mom had told her how I'd disappointed her. But Julia, a quiet, nonjudgmental presence, drove me to the Footlocker.

I felt the anxiety as I planned my first outing. I had to put those socks on myself. I had to fasten the casts so that they'd fit properly and then attach them to the special slippers to get into the car. I needed to transfer myself into that wheelchair in the parking lot. It was a long trek to the Footlocker. Purse on my lap, I let Julia push me from the parking garage into the mall. Attached to IV's just a few weeks ago, I timidly entered the real world.

A teenage sales boy, wearing a Patriots' jersey, watched me maneuver the wheelchair over to the men's sneaker display. Men's were wider than women's for my still swollen feet. I told the boy I'd just had surgery.

"Cool," he replied.

I told him my size in women's and he figured out what that would be in men's. I asked him to grab one size larger, just in case.

I transferred to a store chair from the wheelchair so I could try the sneakers on and stand up and walk with the crutches. It was quite the scene with casts off, wheelchair parked and crutches by my side. I was oddly proud. Peggy Cook: warrior back from the battlefield. I didn't need to hide. I had had surgery. "Surgery," a term everyone could relate to. It wasn't some religious jargon.

The boy found a pair of white and blue high tops, not too painful to pull on. Out of the casts' prison, my straight feet felt freedom. Room to move.

I laughed when he asked if I'd like to wear them home, like some 6 year-old. Nope, just a bag for them would do. I couldn't believe I had found sneakers that fit so easily. All my life I had to try myriad shoes or sneakers to find ones that just might stay on and not cause blisters.

Julia asked if we should stop for lunch on the way home, but I was too exhausted from my sneaker purchase. I couldn't imagine maneuvering in a restaurant.

A surge of emotion hit me as I rested on the bed when I got home. I often experienced surges of happiness and sadness at the same time. The kindness of others, the energy draining convalescence. I'd cry and then make myself stop. I didn't want the boys toddling by, noticing their semi-helpless aunt weeping. My feelings, still a mix of guilt, joy, fear, and anticipation.

I didn't have a therapist yet. I didn't know I needed one.

That next Saturday was the first one in months that I didn't go to Dr. Z.'s office to have new casts made. I'd be wearing my bivalve casts until I got the "all clear" to try walking in my new sneakers. Instead Dr. Z. called and told me to put my sneakers on, and take a few steps with my crutches. There were no cell phones in those days where he could observe. We hung up and I prepared for this next "step."

My brother was home that day and I asked him to stand nearby. I pulled the socks on and then tackled the sneakers. As I stood up, I had a unique sensation in my ankles. I was sure this was not good. My feet, even though the ankles were fused, had some give. I could flex the ankles ever so slightly. Something my old ankles never experienced. I told my brother I thought I had broken something.

He just stared at me. He didn't think so.

I had never been able to flex in the slightest. How could I flex if I was fused? Standing flat with newly formed heels, not in a cast, was also a first. But that slight movement in the ankles totally freaked me out. Dr. Zimbler hadn't mentioned any movement like that.

David and I decided I should call Dr. Z. back and ask just in case something had snapped. What did I know about straight feet and reconstructed ankles?

The receptionist patched me right through.

When I told Dr. Z. how the ankle had some give, he replied, "That's what ankles do, dear." I will hear his sweet reassurance forever.

I wish I had kept a journal or diary. But at that time, I was self-conscious even with myself. I couldn't put anything down on paper that I might read, or God forbid, someone else might find. All the memories are stored inside me. The exciting little victories and scary setbacks. I dream about them still. I have flashbacks.

I did something for me, without permission.

HOME

Joy is always on time.

Maggie Smith

It was time to leave. I'd been at David's since mid-April. Now, it was mid-July. I got the "going home" inspiration and perhaps even the subliminal message from Matt. Lying on the living room couch, I watched Linda bring up clean clothes from the dryer to pack in the suitcase on the floor. She and the boys were getting ready for their yearly trip to Bay Head, New Jersey.

Her family owned an oceanside cottage there. Myriad young cousins gathered each summer for "together time." Linda loved catching up with her three sisters for an entire month. Swimming, footlong sub sandwiches, crashing waves. David, never a beach person and ultra-busy with his work, always drove his family to the shore, and then went back to Boston until the next weekend. Then he'd drive down again for the weekends. I imagined David relished time at home alone after workdays as managing editor for *The World Monitor* nightly news program.

"Are you sure you'll be okay if I drive them down and you'll be alone for the day?" David asked.

I was tremendously excited to have this kind of freedom for the first time in months—even though I'd not be leaving the inside of their house. Yet anyway.

As Linda continued stacking clean clothes in the suitcase, Matt, 3, came into the living room. Linda went back down to retrieve more clothes and Matt gave me an eye.

A sideways glance. An "I bet you won't believe when I do this" look. But I taught so I knew "looks" and sideways glances from little boys.

Matt walked over to the suitcase and began to jump up and down with gusto on the clean clothes. The organized stack of clothes fell over, and the suitcase wobbled back and forth. He looked at me. He knew his mom was nearby.

What did I want to say? What *should* I say? Two different questions.

Just the fact that I was thinking of what to say illustrated the progress of my recuperation. Thinking of something other than my feet and my discomfort felt novel.

I looked him in the eye, and said, like a kindly aunt, not a teacher, "Matt, your sneakers are going to get the clothes dirty and you might destroy the suitcase." Blaming it on the sneakers, not the headstrong boy wearing the dirty sneakers.

He stared at me, smirking. He jumped with even more force.

"Did you hear what I said?" I asked a bit more seriously but not so much that I overstepped my bounds as the forever-present houseguest. He stared at me again, tongue in cheek, and kept jumping.

His mom rounded the corner, "Matt, get out of that suitcase now. And with your sneakers on, what are you doing?"

Matt stepped briskly out of the suitcase.

He turned his face towards me and gave me a "See, I don't need to listen to you" glare.

For some reason something clicked inside me. I think, possibly, I had hurt feelings. I thought we were buddies, kindred spirits. That part was right. Buddies. For some reason I thought he'd remember I was a teacher and respond accordingly. When I said "stop" at school, my word became law. But why would I expect him to think of me as an authority figure?

I was still a bit emotional, just weaning off my Percocet and all. On the other hand, at this point I was so ready to go home that this event gave me the signal to go. I had weeping gratitude daily for every bit of help I received. I still had gratitude, but I needed my autonomy again, at least in living accommodations.

At lunch I told Linda and David I thought I was ready to go home and would ask friends to come get me the next weekend. I'd need two friends, one to drive me home, and the other to drive my car back to my house. My burgundy Honda waited patiently in David's driveway for four months. I knew just whom I'd ask. Sherry and Sue had told me if I needed anything at any time to call. And for a weekend move, they'd be free. I needed them, for sure.

David and Linda didn't try to change my mind. It must have been a relief for them to know that after the trip to NJ, their house would be theirs again. No hospital bed, wheelchair, or commode. No doctor appointments a half hour away. No strangers in their house providing PT and blood tests. Nobody listening in and watching parenting and coupling discussions.

I know I'd never want someone in my house for four months, especially a family member. A helpless one at that. I'd been the weekend caregiver for my mom for too many years. It had worn me down. I tended to care too much. Watching pain sent my empathy into overdrive. It was a heavy weight to not be able make things better for my mom. At that point in my life, I never thought I'd be able to take care of anyone again.

I was super psyched to think of being in my cozy home. Newburyport, the ocean, friends nearby. I had just moved from my apartment to the tiny duplex I had bought four years before when I began the medical adventure. I had watched its construction and chosen all the colors, inside and out. I felt a wave of relief and excitement.

In my own home, I could be pathetic or happy without anyone observing my unsteady emotions. There'd be obstacles for sure. Going up and down two floors. There's a living room/kitchen/dining room but no bathroom on the first floor. It was probably 20 steps up to the second floor to my bedroom, a study, and the bathroom. The washing machine and dryer were another 10 steps down from the living room into the basement. I'd need to be so careful using the crutches on the stairs. Maybe I could just toss the laundry bag and slide down the stairs on my bum.

I'd only been walking for a couple of weeks. School started in a month. I had to get on with it.

When I called Dr. Z. to ask if he thought I was ready for the transition to my home, he asked how my house was set up? He gave me permission but admonished me not to overdo it, and that meant only going up and down the stairs twice a day. I decided I'd pack a lunch after breakfast downstairs and then not come down again until dinner.

I was not driving yet, and my Honda was a stick shift. That could be troublesome. How would I get to Dr. Zimbler's for checkups? I still went every other week to make sure "we were moving in the right direction."

Just get me home.

I called Sherry and she called Sue and the move was a go. Sherry said she'd be my driver for as long as I needed. Sue said she'd be my grocery shopper attendant indefinitely. My Newburyport cheerleaders, teaching comrades and best friends. They had both been in constant contact with me during the recuperation. Sherry had visited me every weekend. She brought letters from my class, news from the teachers' room, and a companionship I looked forward to each Saturday. She never missed one weekend.

I called Sue, who no longer taught, every morning at 11:00 during my hospitalizations. Eleven, the bewitching hour before 12:00 when my next meds arrived. By 11:00, I was climbing the walls with pain and worry. She'd tell me what her young children had been doing. She'd tell me some tale of her husband Jeff's hiking or home repairs. What Basil, their black lab, had gotten into recently. Basically she talked to me for an hour, while I writhed in bed until the nurse came in. Then I thanked her and hung up.

Sherry and I both taught first grade and had become fast friends. We carpooled, which gave us time to talk shop and to get to know each other. For so long when I had period cramps, she'd tell me to consider taking Motrin. Not obnoxiously, just incredulous that I'd suffer like that every month. Of course I declined, knowing prayer was more effective.

When I told her during one ride to school that I was pondering surgery, flabbergasted was her reaction. I also detected excitement that I'd be joining the real world.

Every step of the way, from blood work to donating blood for my procedure to calming my fears to learning to swallow iron pills, Sherry and Sue counseled me. We also could laugh with the sheer absurdity of all the new skills I was learning that the rest of the world took for granted. Who doesn't know how to swallow pills? Water in a cup, pill in mouth, gulp of water. When I first knew I'd need health care, they told me how to notify the front office, assuring me they wouldn't laugh at my arrested development. I had been teaching for 10 years but had relied on Christian Science for any kind of healing. No doctor visits, no prescriptions.

I was scared to tell the principal I'd need some months off. Sherry and Sue assured me that my walking was important. That the principal cared about her staff. And they were right.

Sherry and Sue were on call to listen and assured me my upcoming surgery was a stupendous idea. I'd never talked about my feet to them before, but now I became an open book for worries, fears, and traumatic stories from my past. Talented listeners, truly a gift. The two of them were my first school friends to come visit at the hospital the day after my first surgery. I was still in a morphine haze, crying and laughing incoherently. They told me once I was back walking again how worried they were during that first visit, how they exuded joy and lightheartedness but in the parking lot, they cried. Agony is never easy to watch.

I knew they'd be great movers with that go-to teacher attitude. I didn't have that much to move. A duffel bag with clothes. I threw out my old sneakers. It was a strange feeling to leave them behind, like my old feet. I wore my new high tops now. I had a couple of pillows plus books and tapes of my favorite hymns. I played them nightly during my midnight to 5 am insomnia. I packed my projects and games, which I never had the concentration to use. A wall calendar, each day since April crossed out. Stacks of get-well cards that I saved in a large plastic bag to reread and my hospital discharge papers to file at home.

They arrived in Sue's station wagon on Saturday. Just to hear their voices in person made me feel normal again. I was no longer just an invalid. It was back to having friends, back to laughter, back to a bit of confidence that my new life finally had some momentum.

Sherry drove my car and I drove in the station wagon with Sue, with me sitting in the back seat to stretch out. Off we went up 95 North. Now I was heading in the right direction. As each town sign appeared, my anticipation grew. A thrill, but also sobering, knowing I'd need to conserve my energy for day-to-day tasks from now on.

A major milestone. I had fantasized about this trek for months. Here it was. I had survived. Now on to round two.

Finally, there it was. My little duplex. I owned the left side. The driveway seemed steeper than before. It would not be fun exiting the car and trying to climb the steep slope on crutches. So I walked sideways. I'd need practice later walking in the right direction. Up the front steps with both crutches under one armpit, the other hand grabbing the wrought iron railing.

Sue and Sherry kept saying, "Take your time."

I kept saying, "I'm fine!"

Newburyport. Not a suburb, a small city. A city on the Merrimac River and the Atlantic Ocean. If the breeze blew in a certain direction, I smelled the ocean and listened to the seagulls call. I lived on a main drag and I loved it. The cars whizzed past, the lawn mowers drowned out neighbors chatting. Cats ran across the street trying to avoid disaster. I lived alone but I felt surrounded, in a good way.

Sue and Sherry carried in my belongings. God, now what? The exhaustion from the ride and anticipation suddenly grabbed me. We'd planned to go grocery shopping right then to fill my empty refrigerator. But good friends knew what made sense. The color drained from my face, an obvious hint. Sue told me she'd come back in a few hours and we'd go then. My next-door duplex neighbors, Chris and Mike, stopped in and offered any help any time. They were a young couple with a toddler, Ken. I had always kept a shy distance from them. But they always made an effort to chat in the front yard as I came home from errands. Each year I received an invitation to their Christmas open house, but I'd never attended. As usual my reply was "I'm fine, thanks."

I hoped the answer didn't sound unfriendly. I was used to privacy, keeping my cards close to my vest. I always wanted to appear competent. They seemed ready for this response and didn't push. I appreciated knowing they were next door if I got in a jam. And just the sound of Ken running around in their half of the duplex kept me company more than once.

I'd been slowly learning humility during my recuperation. It took practice to consistently find the words to ask for help. I never wanted to be a burden. I'd learned that, just like with Dr. Z., no one in my new world expected perfection. I had to remember that.

Sherry offered to give me driving lessons. I'd been driving since I was 16. Now I had new scaffolding. My foot shape had totally changed.

I had adapted to my feet facing in so as not to hit the wrong pedals. With my stick shift, I'd need to relearn how to maneuver the clutch from my knees down not with just the ball of my foot. The new movement, using my heel and toes, needed to be automatic while driving. As coordination was not my forte, I'd need to learn to use these new appendages while keeping my eyes on the road.

I had tons to do in the meantime. I needed to call the visiting nurse to set up a PT evaluation. I'd have to see if I could get a wheelchair for maneuvering in the kitchen. There was no way I'd be able to make my own meals standing up yet. I'd had brief second thoughts amazed by my lack of energy for making a simple cheese sandwich. But thank God for props like wheelchairs, crutches, and bannisters. I needed to figure out how to get my garbage cans to the end of my driveway each Friday morning.

Sherry and Sue left, and I lay on the couch, looking around the living room in blissful awe. I'd finally made it home. I slept for a few hours, after dragging myself upstairs to use the bathroom. This house was not set up for post-surgery. Yet in spite of the awkward floor plan, I felt a surge of power. Sometimes I scootched around on my butt. Sometimes my crutches were my best friends. I decided to call the visiting nurse office in our city and left a message about a loaner wheelchair and physical therapy.

Peggy Cook, a person again, not a patient.

I could do this. I'd endured the unknown before. I'd even more possibilities starting today. I'd be so much more outgoing now. Nothing to hide, right? No need to be so cautious. Maybe I'd try dating. Maybe I'd go back to my church and they'd be so impressed with my new feet, they'd never look at me askance for going the medical route.

How could new physical scaffolding begin to leach into my psyche and change my emotional scaffolding? How long would it take? How could I go from the fearful introvert in social situations to a party girl? I'd always wanted to be a party girl. To saunter into a room and talk to random strangers. Maybe even a man. To keep a conversation going after the "What do you do for a living?" To be up for adventures, not hiding in my home, my safe cave.

Sue and Sherry made a big impact on me in this regard. Sue was a natural extrovert, a happy person. Certain she was faking it, I kind of resented her smiling all the time. But as I got to know her, she genuinely had a positive attitude. She wasn't afraid of people. She laughed robustly at the ridiculousness of kids' behavior at school. She was a creative artist, not afraid to share her needlepoint, her weaving, her sewing, her crafts. Her husband was equally open. They were into enjoying life.

I watched how they dealt with their little girl, Stephanie, who'd been born with her hips out of joint. No panic. No worries that the infant wore a cumbersome brace for months. Happy to explain the condition to staring onlookers. Life went on without a hitch. No praying, no feeling guilty, no pity. Just joy in their precious newborn. Such a contrast to my experience of being different. Their behavior impacted my thinking. How did they become this way? Was this unique just to them?

When I called Sue on the phone and her husband answered, I'd shyly say, "Hi, Jeff, it's just Peggy. Is Sue home?" She's in the other room." Then I'd hear him yell, "Hey, Sue, it's just Peggy." Somehow that loosened me up and helped me feel less self-conscious and less of a bother, needing to apologize for existing.

Watching their relationship taught me a lot about what I wanted in life. A companion. A companion who wasn't degrading. "Happy" looked like fun. An energy seemed to express, "We are mentally healthy."

Sherry taught me that every day was not a crisis. She didn't seem full of anxiety or gloom. Sick? Go to a doctor. Difficult child? Try new strategies. New curriculum? Dive in. Demanding parent? Call and talk, then let it go. Impressive to a person who woke up each morning fretting.

Socially Sherry seemed at ease, an extrovert. Going to parties with her boyfriend, the ship builder, vacations in Japan, concerts in Boston, even on weekdays. And shockingly she also she wanted to hang out with me. One summer morning she came to my apartment unannounced and asked if I wanted to go to the beach. The beach? With my feet? She seemed oblivious to my physical deficits. Sue seemed that way too.

I never had taken much notice of people unless they were Christian Scientists. Only people in the religion could be role models. Others didn't seem to have much in common with me if they went to doctors, drank, or took meds. I didn't feel at home with people "like that." I needed to spend huge amounts of time praying, just so I didn't go totally off the deep end, trying to be so damn perfect. Now I broke out of my prayer cocoon when I hung out with Sue and Sherry. I wondered if I could join their world. I watched these friends living life, enjoying it, and finding humor. It opened me to new possibilities. I became more at home with others and perhaps even myself. I'd go to Sue and Jeff's for a Trivial Pursuit competition. I gulped when I saw all the cars in front of their house, but I took a deep breath and walked in. I spent many Saturdays at the Children's Museum bookstore with Sherry looking for good early readers. We sussed out recycling factories for our classroom art areas: two bags for five dollars. She and I had similar passions.

Yes, my mom's death caused me to look the religion "in the eye." At the same time these friendships gave me positive role models for a possible future. Even now with the post-surgery challenges.

But I wasn't alone. It was no longer just God and me. I had Dr. Z, my physical therapist, my school friends. I had a network. David and Linda called often to check on me. I finally let others, not just God help and guide me. My relationship with God was no longer the only relationship I had. Yes, I still recited hymns during sleepless nights. I'm not sure if the hymns proved I still believed in God or if they were beautiful poetry that I had known forever. I thought perhaps I'd go back to church again, but I had plenty of time to ponder that. It didn't need to happen right away.

In fact none of my church friends even knew I was home. I hadn't told them my plans. I didn't feel estranged from God or them at my arrival. I had too much to do to give the church much thought. Time to mentally wrestle with my belief in God and loyalty to the religion would come later. On that arrival date, I felt elation, gratitude, and fatigue.

My ride home that July was a car ride up the highway to my physical home. I was coming home to a new way of being. Starting to see myself as a person, not a condition. A person who had a life to rebuild. A person no longer imprisoned by a dead-end prognosis.

My physical changes began to morph my inner desires and thoughts about new positive possibilities. Maybe I'd go camping, maybe I'd walk in the woods near home. Maybe I'd ride a bike again.

Maybe I'd host a party at my house. An ever-present doom dissipated. Home became more than a zip code.

I became more at home in my physical body as the recuperation continued and PT began in full. I learned to balance on my new heels, to enter a store with confidence. I was strangely proud of my walking now, even though with crutches and unsteady gait. In the grocery store if someone saw me walking down the aisle with crutches and asked, "Oh dear, what happened to you?" I smiled and answered, "I had my clubfeet fixed." I didn't wait to explain further. I had taken command of my "problem," as we used to call it in my family. I stood up straight, perhaps with pride.

My new physical scaffolding slowly helped rebuild my inner scaffolding.

After surgery I gradually began to see the disconnect in living a prescribed way of life versus a life that considered my needs. I craved the freedom and creativity to craft something new and whole. I had taken the first step by going to the hospital.

During the next four years, through progress and setbacks, I slowly reshaped my life. That coming home day in July was a perfect beginning. A rebirth.

My renaissance.

PART V

THE TRANSFORMED

STANDING TALL

He never mentioned braces. He omitted that in my pre-surgery appointments. The aftermath of reconstructive surgery had so many unknowns, ones I could never have imagined when I interviewed Dr. Z. about taking my case. In my naïve mind I only considered the physical aftermath and not very accurately: relearn how to walk, wear fancy shoes. The end. Instead, the physical recovery was just the beginning and multi-faceted. The spiritual aftermath hadn't been visualized yet.

Each night for the next 18 months, I drove myself to physical therapy at the local hospital. I felt honored to qualify for such intensive, free help from professionals. I never considered it a drag. I used to hate any 1:1 attention to my physical body. The shame, a constant taunt only I could hear. Now I looked forward to each session. These people knew what they were doing. I could feel it. They had a plan for my future walking.

My gait became less unsteady in those nightly sessions. My feet began to feel connected to the rest of my body. I lay on the table, a sheet up to my neck, looking at the ceiling, while the PT dug her elbows into my hip joints and kept the pressure on with the weight of her body until she felt the hip loosen or "give." I learned hips mattered. They helped me keep my balance and let my legs move freely. "Myofascial release" was a new dreaded term. When I stood up, though, my body seemed taller and looser.

"You are so tight," she'd admonish each night. "Lie on your dining room table on your back with your legs hanging over the edge at least once a day," she suggested. *Who does that,* I thought? But I kept my window blinds shut and complied.

The overall physical progress was obvious. My feet rotated and flexed much more than right after surgery. I had never wanted anyone touching my feet, especially with my socks off. The shape of my feet repelled me and others, I was sure. In this setting, however, everyone was so impressed by the transformation from clubbed to semi-normal shape that I soon got over that automatic hiding behavior. Medical personnel had a clinical view, not judgmental like mine had always been. They were actually excited to see a case like this. I was the poster child for a triple arthrodesis surgery in an adult.

Pretty soon I'd walk through the physical therapy door, still on crutches, like an old pro. I'd step on the step stool to get on my assigned table and immediately take off my sneakers and socks. I'd drop them to the floor. The PT, her hands always warm, held one foot at a time and asked me to wiggle one toe, then the other. This was the nightly warm-up. I learned to isolate movements in each toe, to try to get up and down movement or range of motion back where there had been none. Post-surgery nerve damage was expected to some degree, but as yet, we did not know how permanent. The PT's hands were always as gentle as Dr. Z's. I felt at home.

I learned to look up. In the past, I hated people staring at me, so I avoided eye contact. Now I needed to walk with purpose and confidence, not schlep along like an untouchable. Since Dr. Z.'s only admonition so far was "don't fall," looking up became mandatory. Head up, I saw the office doors in this little city hospital, the artwork on the walls, the photos of the heads of departments lining the entranceway of Anna Jacques Hospital. The phlebotomists walked around with blood-taking carriers, vials clanking. The switchboard operator began to wave to me each night. I waved back, no longer fixated on the linoleum flooring.

The pain, controlled by the TENS machine at the end of each PT session and the anti-inflammatories I took each morning, were a Godsend. The TENS machine, massive and computer-like, sat on a rolling cart next to where I was lying. Electrodes attached to each ankle sent pulsating charges that lessened the pain. Soon I applied for a prescription for a compact TENS machine that fit in a small tote bag. It was a good way to start the morning before school and right after. I loved that I owned this marvelous device. Pain buzzed away temporarily. No mandated prayer.

At school, I taught in high top sneakers with crutches. The lunch ladies cheered me on each day as I dropped my class off at noon. How amazing, they exclaimed. How the feet faced forward, how I smiled out of the blue. The women marveled. I had taught many of these women's children in the past. They knew me when my feet faced each other. They knew me when I didn't look adults in the eye unless it was report card conference time. I felt like saying "Hi" as I entered the school kitchen and the teachers' room. A new breeze had blown in, a breeze that lessened my paranoia and depression.

The teachers helped me feel accomplished for making it through the morning in a bustling first grade classroom, stopping in to see if I needed help with anything. Some stood in the hall and just said, "Wow" as I walked by. When I made it to the top of the steps waiting to get into the auditorium for an assembly, some of the kids from other classrooms commented, "Great walking, Miss Cook."

I couldn't stand on the desks yet to reach stored materials or decorate for Halloween. So I appreciated other teachers' nimble bodies hopping up and doing the job for me as we chatted. I never had to ask. Sometimes they offered to take the kids up to the bus for me at the end of the day. They knew me well enough to see that look in my eyes.

Just three more hours to go, I'd tell myself each noon. And what a relief taking more meds at lunch. I loved my Motrin. So much easier than gritting my teeth in pain like I used to do in the "olden" days with period cramps.

There was some sitting during the day, but not a lot. Teaching reading to small groups, I could sit at the long rectangular table, with the kids facing me. Reading chapter books after recess in the black rocking chair, a reprieve. Taking it easy during the end-of-the-day art project/activity time.

In between the sitting there was the walking. On linoleum. Cement underneath. Constant walking. Back and forth to set up for science experiments. Checking math work one-on-one at the tables. Walking around the room to give attention to each seating group. Refilling paint pots, checking to see whose boots were still in the hall before recess. Cleaning the rabbit cage. Lugging new wood shavings to the cage from the closet. Cleaning up spills and overturned glue in the art area. Lining up and walking to the gym, music, art, and library. Picking them up at the end of their enrichment classes. Traipsing to bus lines on the first floor at the end of the day from my basement classroom. Monitoring the halls as the children waited impatiently and the volume rose. "Inside voices and keep your hands to yourself," we implored.

When the school cleared each afternoon, I'd put my feet up on my desk, breathe deeply and rest. It took energy to pack up my bag filled with papers to correct and drive home.

"Extreme fatigue by 2 or 3 pm, lack of stamina," I reported to the PT. Partially from the long hours. Partially from the all-day use of my new feet. My Achilles tendons, newly lengthened, ached. Before surgery I'd used my hips to jet forward. I torqued my hips and back out of whack for decades. Now my hips, knees, legs, and feet needed strengthening to do their individual jobs to lead my feet forward. Both calves atrophied from my clubfeet, so each day was an intense rebuilding process. Stamina is earned, not a gift.

Each night in PT I learned to use the correct body parts for propulsion. Hips and backs don't walk. Legs and feet do. Unlearning old habits, we built new muscles endlessly. Walking in front of mirrors. Roaming the hallways of the hospital to build a smooth gait. Walking up the cement stairs to see steadiness improve with crutches.

At a checkup in the late fall, the PT and I both reported to Dr. Z. that the pain level by the end of the day teetered on the "unbearable." Somewhat normal, he commented, considering the bodily adjustment. Then Dr. Z. wondered out loud if I needed special shoes with metal braces to help stabilize my entire body and also to take on some of the work of dorsiflexion.

Dorsiflexion is when your foot moves up and down to clear stairs and keeps you from shuffling and tripping. I now had it, by virtue of my new heels, but I didn't know how to use my heels for my walking benefit.

When he mentioned BRACES, I immediately thought, *Oh, no, it's not* that *bad.*

But the jig was up and Dr. Z. wanted to avoid putting too much pressure, too quickly, on the new feet and ankles. He needed my feet, now with heels, and my legs to work together as a unit for life. No one area should do more of the work than another, he said.

So off to the brace/shoe/orthopedic center I went, prescription in hand, late one afternoon after school. The ancient building with its sagging roof, off of Rt. 495, sat in a deserted industrial park looking grim. I couldn't believe Z. had recommended this place. But I was used to trusting him and parked the car as close to the entrance as possible.

Sometimes I felt like my recuperation was going backwards, getting more paraphernalia than I'd ever had. Dr. Zimbler, though, looked at this hardware as a way forward, a bit of support for the "new structure" gaining strength. So I revamped my thinking to be less judgmental about my efforts. Each body is different, he reminded me. I was older doing this process, he encouraged. He thought probably in a year or two, I'd not need them anymore if I kept up with the PT and didn't overdo. I couldn't even consider a year or two at this point.

The building looked like a repurposed factory. A small sign by the front door announced, New England Orthotics and Prosthetics. I quickly learned the magical work going on inside. I waited for my turn in the small waiting room, sitting in a beat-up movie theater chair. Little children with cerebral palsy waited to get new plastic braces after a growth spurt. Children in wheelchairs, their feet and legs braced to the knees. Floppy bodies, tilting heads, sweet smiles. Parents tending to their children's needs, looking like they had been through the wringer.

My technician, a lanky fellow with an amputated leg and foot, wore a prosthesis. At that moment I didn't feel sorry for myself anymore. He read the prescription that I brought and pulled out a pair of brown shoes for me to try on. I sat on a grubby plastic chair. No fancy introductions.

Back to the ugly brown shoes of my childhood. Not high tops at least.

He explained the metal braces attached to each shoe and two leather straps snugly wrapped around the metal. They'd be custom-made for me. He told me about the special hinge put into the shoe/brace that would help lift my ankle up each time I walked. Dorsiflexion assistance. It would take some of the load off my newly weight-bearing feet. Quite fascinating really. He explained the process so clearly. Obviously he had been doing this for years. He said he did a lot of work for Dr. Zimbler. Kids with clubfeet, spina bifida, and cerebral palsy.

He knew all about clubfeet. It was not some embarrassing condition I had to explain. He looked at my still-healing scars. "Dr. Zimbler does such beautiful work," he remarked. I didn't have to explain to him which parts of my legs and feet hurt. It was obvious to him. Another master in his art.

He had all kinds of instruments in his little musty cubicle: wooden hammers, screwdrivers, large wrought-iron scissors. Metal strips, leather, and padding. Long rolls of Velcro.

I thought I'd be done with special footwear after surgery. But this "artist" acted like braces were the obvious next step. A positive aftermath. The brown shoes, with orthotics built in on the inside, could further help stabilize my gait. He made impressions for them right then, as I stood barefoot, on hot foam. "Orthotics," another new vocabulary word.

He tried on a sample pair of shoes to gauge the sizing. The leather, so supple and comfortable, even without the orthotics in them yet. I was quite taken by the luxury of it all in a strange way. I'd never get blisters with these.

Of course, I wouldn't. I had heels now.

He'd build the metal braces/straps and attach the braces to each shoe. They'd be ready in three weeks. Insurance covered some. Insurance, another wonderful invention I'd never benefitted from. Then again, I'd never been in this position with "orthopedic trappings" before. I remember a family friend paying for my casts as a child. And that was as far as we went.

I'd be left with $800 to pay. Luckily they took Master Card. I slid off the table and, walking by that same waiting area, hobbled to my Honda.

Each new appointment was efficient and professional and exhausting. Empathy was always the norm from the professionals. It caused me to feel a tiny smidge of self-compassion. Maybe I'd stop flogging myself for my myriad deficiencies I laser-focused on.

How to be so skilled in helping others walk? Just walk. There's a niche for everyone. Such important niches that daily news reports ignore. Workers and designers in a one-story sagging roofed building, helping others with mobility.

And then the day came to pick up my new armor. They stood tall. All on their own. Rugged-looking. Totally symmetrical. Just what I needed. They grabbed on to their mission with ease.

Metal rods against each side of my leg from the knee down, thick leather straps surrounded them. Industrial brown shoes attached to each brace. Ready for deployment. Attached to each shoe was a hinge that snapped up and down as I walked. That up and down movement of dorsiflexion. The up-and-down, heel-to-toe movement of a foot that comes naturally to most. With each snap of the hinge, I knew I was not alone in my recovery.

The hinge can be set by the technician or doctor to give just a little flip or a big one. Each time I went to see Dr. Z., he'd assess my walking and adjust the hinge to give me less help, but still support, as my legs and feet grew stronger. The hinge made a little tapping sound when I walked, like the tap shoes I'd always wanted. It was no secret when I was approaching around the corner.

There was a sightless girl in our school. One day I entered the girls' bathroom because it was closer than the ladies room. As I clip clopped into the bathroom, Maeve piped up from her stall, "Hi, Miss Cook."

The braces became quite a point of interest in my classroom. Usually my pants concealed the braces. But when I read a chapter book to the kids after lunch and was sitting in the rocking chair, the pants rode up a bit. And there was all that metal and leather and Velcro. What first grader would not be interested in this?

I could see them eyeing the hardware. So I took off one of the braces/shoe and stood it up all by itself. "Cool" was the response from my audience. Then I showed them how the metal on each side supported my leg that was just learning how to walk in a new way. The best part of this show and tell was when I showed them how the shoe could move up and down with the help of the magical hinge.

I no longer winced at "feet" questions, and they had many. Strangely I didn't feel conspicuous for my differences anymore. It was a time to be proud. To show the kids hard work is worth it.

Do the braces hurt? Will I wear them forever? Who made them? Can they touch the brace/shoe structure?

We passed the contraption around the circle. Many oohs and aahs. Heavier than they imagined. Many stories about grandparents who use canes, wheelchairs. Many stories about broken bones. First graders are professional digressers.

I told them I'd eventually not need the crutches. How much longer, they wanted to know. Unknown, I told them. Just depends how I progress. Eventually I'd graduate to a cane., and then walk with the braces all by myself. And someday no braces. The big reward.

Kind of like learning to read, I explained. First the alphabet, next their sounds, then the words, finally the book. The whole story is yours.

Bingo. They got it.

When I arrived home, I stood my hardware by the front door. Ready for duty the next morning.

My Delayed Adolescence

My mind had always zeroed in on straight feet. *The* criterion for a "normal life." Straight feet, the cure-all. How else to define "normal" besides inhabiting a body without deformities? Renewed spiritual energy? Embodying normalcy? How does a person "embody normalcy?" I pieced my life together day by day after surgery.

I had weak survival strategies in the outside world, still locked in childhood, always asking others for permission, what to think, what to do. Since childhood I'd been plowing through hard things, like marching in band, gym class, going on stage to pick up my diploma. Fortitude, always expected by my parents. Remember, my feet were "beautiful," and "perfect." But a gripping inner fear of life still churned inside. It seemed a heady task to move permanently away from "child."

Adolescence. I needed one.

At first I told myself I must focus solely on my physical recuperation, the outer scaffolding. My inner scaffolding, under construction. My soul and spirit came last, I thought. But maybe not. Maybe I'd try integrating my inner scaffolding with my outer. In the mirror I saw a tad more confident me. Not just my straightened feet, my sense of hope and opportunity. The body began to enliven the spirit. So many new ways to "move" in life.

Dr. Z. wanted to know if the daily fatigue and pain improved when I wore the braces. I appreciated the braces for the flexibility they gave me. I switched from sneakers to the braces, on and off, during the day. Sometimes I gave my feet a rest (sneakers) or extra support (braces). My rubbery legs never knew what they wanted. If I wore sneakers, I felt like my legs might give out. If I wore the braces too long, I felt stiff and loaded down by all that metal.

By lunch, I dreaded the afternoon. Math, science, activity time, bus duty. Too much. So the braces were not a cure-all, as nothing is in such a complex recovery. Stamina still didn't come roaring back.

Several times Sherry found me at my desk during lunch crying. I showed her my swollen left ankle. She repeatedly told me full-day teaching was still too much for me.

It hadn't been in September. But then in December, the fatigue and pain had accumulated. I had never been a shirker. Being out three months for surgery during the last school year, although necessary, made me feel like a bum. I HAD to get back to normal that fall. I had always pushed through pain. That was how I grew up. Pain was declared "unreal." But maybe I'd have to search for other ways to cope in order to really grow up.

Dr. Z. had wanted me to take an entire year off from school. Actually he wanted to do one leg at a time with a year in between. I told him that was impossible. But I had never really asked the school their thoughts or told them what my doctor wanted. I always hesitated to make my needs fully known. I felt they were doing enough for me just to let me take three months off with pay. I had to finally leave that scared worthless little girl role and make no apologies. No apologies.

Finally, I talked honestly to the principal. Sherry encouraged me to go up to her office, that minute, eyes still red from crying. My principal had been supportive during the planning of my surgery. But in September, she assumed, if I said I could come back, I felt fine, not that I was willing myself fine. I doubt she realized I had that "no one can do it as well as I can," or that "These are MY kids, only I can teach them the right way" mindset. I started crying the minute I walked into her office, another first.

Stoicism had been the name of my game. Pain is not real; therefore, deny it. Control your feelings. God is your joy. But the rigid self-control had begun to go by the wayside, post-surgery. My legs had more flexibility and I needed to let my soul have the same. My constitution had changed from warrior to mere human. I used to be ultra-hearty, tough; now I always needed a sweater and a tissue. I let down my guard. Yes, I am cold. No, I'm not as tough as I act.

My vulnerability drove me nuts at first. Shocked me. But "get a grip," or "God is my warmth" just didn't work anymore.

We both decided that I'd start to teach half time the next week. The principal called the woman who'd subbed for me during surgery, the most gracious person on this earth and totally competent. So I couldn't resist anymore. I taught reading and writing in the morning. I drove home at lunchtime. Mrs. White taught math and science in the afternoon.

I'd rest at home in the afternoon. I spent hours, yet again, on my bed, feet elevated. Some afternoons, I took a nap. I rarely slept well at night. The night casts I wore to keep my ankles at 90 degrees crashed into each other as I turned over or changed positions. A nap without casts re-energized me for PT at 5 pm.

Around this time in PT, Kate and I seemed to know each other fairly well. For four months I'd been sitting on a table for an hour and a half while she manipulated my feet. We became each other's captive audiences.

Kate's accent was distinctly New England, raised in Newburyport and staying for good. She had wild curly reddish hair, an automatic grin, and a relaxed, can-do manner. Sometimes her hands shook a bit before she started working on my feet. Words just spilled out of her mouth, no filter at all.

Since the regular PT office hours ended at 5:00, we were often the only people in the huge room. Kate had friends all over the hospital, stopping by to chat. She introduced me to the after 5:00 cast of characters. I met Laurie, who worked in transport, and her boyfriend Jay, who worked in maintenance. I met Stella, the switchboard operator who drank her coffee in the PT room during her break. I met all the other PTs who stopped in to pick up their paychecks on Thursdays.

5:00-6:00 pm we concentrated on the serious business of walking, standing up from a sitting position, and stair climbing. As Kate worked on each foot, she told me about her family. How her sister was mentally ill and lived at home. How she drove her crazy. She told me about her married brother and her beloved niece and nephew. She told me about her thwarted love life. She'd dated the town's long-distance runner. I saw him everywhere, long locks streaking behind his emaciated body. How he wouldn't commit to her. I heard all about her new boyfriend, also a PT, who refused to live with her. Kate bought her own little condo instead.

I told her about my sheltered life as a daughter of a church leader. I told her how my mom died of untreated cancer. How everything I had done up to now had been so responsible, so in accord. I told her I'd marched to the religious beat, even when walking became almost impossible. I'd never been so open about my past with a stranger.

So we knew each other. Kind of. I knew her friends, kind of. I thought she was charismatic and young. She was 27. I was 38 almost 39.

Kate, a local girl. Me, a Bostonian. Besides making each other laugh at our messed-up families, there was something else. I didn't know quite what. Perhaps it was the energy of the place. Full of hope. Feeling like I was living in the present. I think I admired Kate, living in the moment with gusto.

6:00-6:30 pm felt like the social hour, while the TENS machine did its thing. Several ex-patients stopped by to show Kate their progress. She flirted with the handsome young men who had crushed their pelvises in motorcycle accidents on Rt. 495. We exchanged war stories. I became the new mascot of orthopedic recovery, as she proudly told all the observers about my clubfoot surgery. I began to be able to talk about my past even with the visitors who stopped in. Now that I had new feet, the story seemed less humiliating. I had finally used my voice, my free will, to change what had been accepted as my fate.

Actually only I had thought of clubfeet as my fate. The rest of the church saw it as unreal and not my fate at all. However, I'd never seen "evidence" of its unreality through spiritual healing of the condition. All my life, my confusion about what was real spiritually vs. what I lived humanly made my brain mush. I felt clearer about my mission since surgery. No longer striving for perfection. Just walk, and try to build a happier life.

Soon, Kate asked if I wanted to go out drinking. Laurie, who usually sat by Kate's side, after her workday, laughed when she asked me that. "Kate, you are her PT."

"Who cares?" said Kate. "She needs to learn how to drink."

So the Grog became our destination. Just the name excited me. I'd been there before with church people to get nachos. But a drink. Yahoo.

So for the first time in my life I looked at an alcoholic drink menu. What's your favorite flavor? Chocolate, of course. Let's get her a Nutty Buddy. Sounded fine to me. An ice cream drink with vodka and Frangelico. I took a tiny sip. Pretty mild. I took some gulps. "Slow down," Laurie said wide-eyed. They were each having some kind of beer.

Wow, that went down fast, I thought.

"You want another?"

"Is it okay?"

"Of course it's okay."

Luckily it was Friday night. After I foggily drove home, I lay on my couch feeling like I might fall off onto the floor. But for sure, it had been THE most fun.

When I told Sherry the next Monday about my time at the Grog, she shuddered. "She's your PT, for God's sake. You're on medication, and she's teaching you to drink?" Actually that did make sense. What was I thinking?

From then on Sherry despised Kate, even though they hadn't met. Every time I told her of Kate's adventures, she told me how no PT behaves like that. "Yeah, you're probably right." But my adolescence had been kick-started.

My responsible best teacher friend: Sherry.

My irresponsible best PT friend: Kate.

So I taught in the morning. Rested in the afternoon. PT/played at night. Never the intent of the afternoons off but that eluded me. I thought it all made perfect sense.

Kate asked if I had been to the iconic restaurant on Rt. 1 with the 20-foot cactus out front. The Hilltop Steak House was a real north shore haunt. I had never even been on the north shore before I got my teaching job. She couldn't believe I'd missed that landmark.

The portions were huge, great big slabs of rare prime rib. I'd seen the long lines outside when I drove down the highway before. But whom would I ever go with? But there we were one Saturday night, in line with the masses. After a 30-minute wait, the waitress led us into the Dakota room. Each room had a western name. Lots of saddles, cowboy hats, wanted posters on the walls, and blaring western music. A bit hoaky but I'd heard the rolls were to die for. Best of all, right across the street sat Kappy's liquor store. Kate and Laurie decided we'd multi-task and set me up with a home liquor bar after dinner.

I never wondered during these outings if they just didn't have dates that night. Did both their boyfriends have something else to do? It never crossed my mind I embodied the Saturday night entertainment or the sociology project. Fun was my only curriculum. I loved every moment.

My eyes were wide open, experiencing new adventures, not tarnished with religious rules. *Why go to a restaurant that serves liquor? We don't want to "support" that kind of establishment.* All my father's platitudes faded.

Full of prime rib we made a U-turn and parked at Kappy's. Walking in I smelled a waft of alcohol. I'd never experienced that aroma before. Shelf after shelf full of beautifully labeled multi-colored bottles greeted me. As an artist, I was enthralled by just the colors. I wanted one of each. I loved glass. But I let Kate and Laurie pick out the must-haves for a beginning bar. I learned certain brands were a must or maybe just their preferences, but what did I know? By the time I checked out I had three boxes of spirits: Bailey's Irish Cream, Frangelico, Absolut Vodka, Jack Daniels, Bacardi Rum and a couple of bottles of white Zinfandel.

They grabbed six packs of Sam Adams and Corona beers. My refrigerator would be stocked for their visits, they explained. Visits? I didn't know I'd be having visits.

I also didn't know what to refrigerate. But Kate and Laurie educated me as we set up the bar in my living room and put the beer in my fridge. When they left, I felt like I'd be able to have normal Saturday night gatherings if I ever got up the nerve.

My first visit ever to a liquor store exhilarated me. But what would David think? Guilt rushed back in after setting up my bar. I decided that very night, I'd do something responsible again. I wrote a letter to the Mother Church asking them to pull my membership. I had been a member since 12, when chronologically I became an adolescent. It's a rite of passage like a Bar Mitzvah. It is the earliest date you can become a member of "the world-wide headquarters of The Christian Science Church."

Because I lived so close to Boston, I had to go into the church offices and interview in person. Mom drove me there just days after my birthday. I met Gordon V. Comer, clerk of the Mother Church. This white-haired elderly gentleman oversaw the membership from all over the world. I remember being so nervous that he'd notice my feet when I walked into his plush office. I wore a red Villager velvet dress, my best. I had pulled on matching tights. I hoped the bright red color would distract him from the shape of my feet. Yet since he was a "healer," maybe it would have been good if he had noticed. At my age he didn't need to ask if I smoke or drank, two of the criteria for membership. He did ask if I relied entirely on CS for healing.

Of course.

So I was invited to be a member, for life. Until I sent that letter. That post-Kappy's liquor store letter.

One afternoon, soon after, as I lay with my feet elevated, I got a phone call from the current clerk of the church, Nate Talbot. He told me gently he'd read my letter of withdrawal and wanted me to reconsider. I felt the blood go up into my head and my stomach began to shake. The tears appeared immediately.

He told me how faithful our family had been. My heart broke and I swallowed sobs. *Don't be kind. I can't take kind.*

I assumed he knew about my mom. Then I told him about me. How I'd hardly been able to walk, but did God care? Mr. Talbot said nothing. I told him I watched my mom die at the BA. Was that proof of God's love? I couldn't believe what was coming out of my mouth. I'd never stood up to a church official before, except my father. I told him I just couldn't do it anymore.

I kind of felt sorry for him. He didn't seem to know what to say. He ended with an invitation to be reinstated if I ever changed my mind. I told him I would never change my mind.

I hung up.

That afternoon, I shocked myself with my verbal courage. I was usually dumbstruck by church officials, the undeserving girl who never got healed. Buckets of tears fell after the call. All the horrendous memories of my mom's suffering swept back in.

Later that afternoon I called my brother to tell him about the call with Mr. Talbot. I was kind of scared he'd get in trouble since David worked for the church as Editor of *The Christian Science Monitor*. I was still in that little girl mindset of "behave yourself, or you'll never get healed."

David said not to worry and he was proud of me. I'd always been so worried about disapproval from authority figures, like a first-grader. That day I had been a mouthy teenager. A normal adolescent.

I'd saved myself, kept myself walking, and wasn't afraid to speak up.

That night in PT I told Kate what I'd done. How could she comprehend what a big step I'd taken? She had gone to Catholic schools so I told her it was like telling off the Archbishop of Boston. She took my mind off that call with a great idea. Maybe I should join Gold's Gym. Right after PT I'd drive over and work out. Just a few days a week.

Now, I'd laugh and say, "What is your problem? I'm supposed be compliant and not overdo." But of course, then I said, "Wow, what a cool idea." I'd never been in a fitness gym. Why would I want to be around sweaty men lifting weights? But Kate said women worked out, too. She suggested I ride the stationary bike and use the StairMaster.

So that very night I drove to the gym and took out a membership. The next night after PT, I had my orientation at Gold's. I told the woman I had just had clubfeet surgery, so I needed to be careful. She had no clue about clubfeet, I could tell by her absent stare. She clicked on the slowest number on the stationary bike and I dropped my crutches and carefully mounted the seat. Mtv was on the overhead screens. I sang along.

My Gold's Gym news almost sent Sherry over the edge. But I had something brand new to think about. The gym. A dream come true. She tried to tell me that Kate was out of her mind. That teaching was plenty for even a half a day. It's counterintuitive to have PT and then work out at the gym right after. "Uh huh." I said.

Thus the pain level basically stayed the same. In the morning I'd be okay. By lunch, my left ankle had a golf ball size bump on it. It was the foot that had the most correction, but it had been the worst to start off with. I pressed on that ankle and felt the water swish around. The medical term: pooling.

I rested in the afternoon.

I'd finish my PT session, and then off to Gold's Gym and cycling. I walked up the moving stairs, grasping the rails. I finally had visions of my physically fit body.

So much for a shorter, less strenuous day.

Of course, did I tell Dr. Z. I was going to the gym? I didn't. I had been so upfront with him about every other feeling and activity I had, but I just couldn't bring myself to disappoint him or disappoint myself by disappointing Kate. Even Laurie said, "Are you sure you should be doing that?"

"Yeah," I said, "Kate said it's fine."

As the months went on, Kate, Laurie and I had more adventures. We even walked right into the Dreadnought, the sleaziest bar in town. Kate and Laurie didn't blink an eye. They introduced me to the bartender as I stared at all the stuffed tunas on the wall, blank eyeballs staring straight ahead.

I felt like a freed hostage. Now that we'd covered restaurants, liquor stores and gyms, next came out-of-state adventures.

A patient offered Kate a condo at Sunday River, Maine, for a weekend. She invited Laurie and me to go. Obviously I had no skis, boots, or intention of going up any hill or mountain.

A snowstorm hit in Massachusetts around 6:30 pm as we left the hospital parking lot. Kate's tires looked a bit bald to me, but she never looked. We piled backpacks in, and Kate and Laurie attached their skis to the roof rack. By the time we crossed the border to New Hampshire, we had white-out conditions. Kate put on her windshield wipers and continued. Laurie wondered out loud if we should turn back.

I was in the back seat sitting side-saddle to keep my feet from pooling. The plows kept the highway passable. We drove in the ruts of other cars. My father would never have approved.

We stopped for gas once. The snow was up to my calves. I will never know how we didn't skid into a ditch that night. I sang hymns to myself, certain they weren't effective after my rude behavior to the church official.

We arrived around 2 am. The light on the ski slopes shone in the distance. Skiing at night, only a fantasy. A scene from a movie. Tricky walking conditions on the packed semi-icy snow. I wore my sneakers and crutches with spikes on the tips for winter traction.

The next day Laurie and Kate skied, and I shopped with all the "beautiful people" in the ski shop. I bought a parka, the kind that skiers wear. CB brand, turquoise, and fitted around the waist. I figured, I deserved it, saving money by not renting skis.

At night they drank at the Sunday River pub, probably hoping to find a boyfriend that would come skiing with them in the future. I wasn't in the mood to sit at a bar with my feet dangling. Too much pressure on my feet. Too much swelling after dangling for hours. I didn't hear when they came back. I was asleep in my sleeping bag, after reading all evening.

That night I began to have a feeling that this might not be the crowd for me. I was here for the ride, but I knew I didn't have too much in common, even with my new liquor purchases. However, I added ski resort to my "fun" resume.

Winters pass slowly in New England, between the blizzards, howling winds, below-zero temperatures, and then finally never-ending slush. It's s one long countdown until spring.

Kate passed the time at her job at the hospital and from time to time showed up after my PT at my house at around 10 pm. She was a little depressed because her boyfriend still didn't want to live with her. She'd come with a few beers already under her belt. I was beginning to recognize the smell of Corona. She wanted to "talk."

I brought out the Fritos.

Getting up at 6:00 am to teach each day, I considered 10:00 pm very late but of course, after all she'd done for me, I listened and listened. Not really knowing what advice to give. I knew nothing about the real her or what she wanted in life. I had never had a boyfriend. So I listened some more and handed her a tissue box.

Finally she asked if she could spend the night. That request unnerved me. I couldn't imagine having someone else breathing in my house at night. I was sure after my mom died, I'd never get attached EVER again to a breathing soul, even though I dreamed of building a family.

Obviously Kate was not going to move in, but panic grabbed me. Logic and equanimity yet to be fully developed in my little excitable mind.

I told myself, "just a night." I had an extra bedroom, showed it to her, and closed the door to my bedroom and went to bed. I left her a note the next morning saying "Lock up and see you tonight at PT."

I didn't like how awkward I felt about the whole thing. But I always felt awkward socially especially if anyone got too close. I used to joke about hating people to invade my space. That meant breathing the same air. I had a slight panic that if someone came into my house, how would I get them out? Now I know that's called *anxiety*.

But after all, she was my PT. After hours she was maybe my friend. Maybe I needed to lighten up. But then again, I'd never show up at one of my student's parents' house at night and ask to talk. Especially if not invited.

Sherry confirmed that this person was not a good example of a PT. Someone who should be guarding my activities, and admonishing me not to overdo and strain my still healing feet and legs. Kate had already led me astray with the Gold's Gym membership, drinking on painkillers, and walking on snow at ski resorts. Then the light dawned on our connection: loneliness.

I'd been lonely forever. My hospital experience had filled some of that void with the hubbub all around me. Dr. Zimbler, the best father figure ever, had my back. He delivered what no other person or religion could. But without my religion and its all-encompassing lifestyle, what did I have left?

My ability to connect with people without panic was a long way off.

Kate was lonely for sure. Her boyfriend was rarely around. She'd been dumped by the other one she really loved. Her family's difficulties sounded really long term and dark. She wanted someone there for *her*. But still I had a feeling something was off. I usually had good instincts. I mean I knew years before, I shouldn't be in my religion. It didn't work for me. So who cares if Kate and I are so different? I was building a new self. Who really knows who I am? And I did like this new self, the one that Kate encouraged. Up for anything and not overthinking every detail. How could befriending a therapist be wrong?

But what was with the unease?

I feared I had inherited my mom's never-ending compassion and maybe her illogical reasoning, Kate wasn't just *a* therapist, she was *my* therapist. She had to have had some kind of professional protocol training.

I tried to be a bit more sensible at Gold's Gym. I stopped with the stair master and switched to hand weights. Shedding the crutches for a cane at the end of spring became my goal. I needed to keep myself on a sensible continuum, not overdoing, nothing to prove. I did my exercises from Dr. Zimbler at home. At PT, I continued to walk the halls and strengthen my leg muscles. My lower leg muscles began to feel sturdier, not on the verge of collapse.

In the meantime, Sue and Jeff moved up to New Hampshire to build a house. Sherry and I visited them on weekends to observe the construction and cheer them on. It felt peaceful, tempering some of the insanity with sensible but still fun "normal" people. The ride to and from New Hampshire gave Sherry and I time to reconnect since I wasn't at school in the afternoons, and evenings I spent at PT and the gym.

Those Saturday visits felt like a homecoming. A homecoming to more ease in my body. I spoke freely and happily, too. I used to be so tongue-tied and uptight even with them. Now I sensed that my life might turn around. Maybe I'd have a family like theirs in the future. I felt like there were options for me finally. I no longer had such a woe-is-me feeling.

I walked with a pretty steady gait around their woodsy lot. Their kids, Steph and Greg, led the way. On those walks I felt like a cane wasn't too far off. Sometimes I held the crutches over my head, triumphant. We all laughed and bantered as we trudged through the woods and around the construction site. Sue told me perhaps she'd be mating Basil, their female black lab. "Would you like a puppy in the future?" she asked. "Think about it. Pick of the litter."

A breathing creature would take some deliberation. A big risk, loving a creature again.

PT continued with Kate, and our after-hours adventures increased. An all-night diner at 2 am. Frequenting drinking dives I'd read about in the local paper in the police blotter. Canoeing down the Parker River with a storm rolling in. Paddling back quickly as thunder approached. Attending healing services at a Catholic retreat center.

I'd mentioned I might be looking for a new religion. But this service was too "out there" in my limited religious mind. Kind of holy-roller. Other methods of healing? Parishioners collapsed on the ground, then declared themselves healed. Not sure I believed that. Incense, candles lit. So different from my austere, no-frills church.

It felt heavenly camping at Hermit Island in Maine, with Laurie and Jay, during Memorial Day weekend. A first-time tent owner, setting up in semi-darkness, still wearing braces. Trekking to the outhouse in the middle of the night making sure not to trip on pine tree roots. Waves crashing in the distance. Suddenly I wanted to camp. My school friends would love it up here.

And then came the summer trip.

Both Laurie and Kate loved driving and thought a trek to Amish Country in Pennsylvania might be fun. I had been once before and was flattered by the invitation. Laurie took care of the logistics. I packed my bag.

On the way I got a strange vibe when we first stopped at Hershey Park. Kate and Laurie piled out of the car to explore, but I told them I'd wait in the car. I wanted to "save my legs" for the Amish Country. I looked forward to the myriad shops there that displayed homemade quilts.

Kate gave me a strange "I don't approve" look. I had never seen that look from her before. But I read and was perfectly happy. They returned in an hour.

After driving through farmland until 5 pm, we found the B and B off a dirt road. I changed into my braces. When we met in the dining room for supper, I again got a look.

Now I was starting to get anxious. Laurie had driven her car so I was a prisoner in Pennsylvania. Old thinking returned. Always on the verge of catastrophe. Run. Escape. Don't face your fears. Instinctively I started singing hymns to myself, a sure sign of impending panic. I ate my dinner and quickly went to my room. I needed to rest, I explained as they set off looking for a package store.

We did some driving and exploring the next day. The bright colored quilts so distinctly Amish flapped in the warm breezes from each store. I didn't buy anything but just looked at the quilts as gorgeous pieces of art. I still got a strange vibe when I'd sit on a bench to rest. But maybe my paranoia about always being the odd one out was the culprit. Then again, maybe I didn't seem as fun as usual. I couldn't sustain fun for more than a few hours at a time. I had to take care of my body. My instincts seemed accurate, even if I didn't always know what to do with them.

More eye-rolling at dinner. Kate only bantered with Laurie. Laurie seemed oblivious.

I called Sherry that night from my room, and like a child, reported the strange vibes. I told her I wanted to come home, but I didn't have my car. She had warned me about going away with them. But she had warned me all along. She is so diplomatic, she'd never say, "I told you so." She knew me enough to know my anxieties, and when they hit, how I wanted to escape. She tried to calm me down and just told me to hang in there. I'd be home the next day.

So that's what I did. I kept pretty quiet, not in a pouty way, but just because I felt like I was on the verge of a bout of diarrhea. I didn't want to further annoy.

Back in Newburyport, PT continued as usual, well not quite. Kate got very quiet for about two weeks. I couldn't put my finger on anything specific that had happened. But I did know she was not joking around as much or chatting as much, actually not at all.

I waited, feeling like the bad girl who had displeased her father. I had experienced the silent treatment in childhood, not knowing what I had done. I didn't dare confront her. Not yet.

Evidently she wasn't afraid in the least to confront me.

One evening as I walked to the car after the PT session. I heard my name. I looked back and as I unlocked my car. Kate came up to the door.

"What's up?" I asked as I slid behind the driver's seat.

"I have to talk to you. I can't be your therapist anymore."

Stunned, I just stared at her. I suddenly was relieved I was in the car and she was not. I could escape if I had to.

"I can't stand working with you anymore. I can't stand touching your feet anymore. We are done."

"What do you mean *done*?" I asked. "What about PT?" My voice sounded quivery and hollow.

"You don't need therapy anymore. You're done."

Suddenly, I used my voice. A big adolescent moment. "Dr. Zimbler tells me when I'm done, not you." And I drove away. Crushed, petrified, and desperate, I drove to Sherry's house. No cell phones in those days. Luckily, Sherry answered the door. We sat on her porch. As always, the adult voice. The voice of calm. The voice of a loyal friend.

I spilled out what had happened in the hospital parking lot.

"This is not your fault," she said.

But I was convinced I had done something very wrong.

"No," she assured me. "She is not a stable person. Call Dr. Z. on Monday and ask for an appointment."

As always Dr. Z. greeted me like my long-lost father. When I explained what had happened (not the trips and late nights) but the sudden dismissal, he offered to call Kate's boss. In total disgust, he declared, "She needs to be fired."

"Please don't do that," I begged.

Then he sweetly asked what I'd like him to do.

"Would you call the supervisor and say I need a new PT? I am not done."

"Done? Of course you're not done. Another 6 months maybe."

I couldn't believe I'd need to go back to the hospital in that room with a new PT. But I was sure I wasn't going to be run out by Kate. I didn't care how scared I was.

My new referral, an assistant PT. One with not as much experience. I didn't complain. I'm sure she had been told Kate's view of the whole situation, whatever it was. But this young woman behaved as professionally as Kate had not.

Sometimes Kate walked back and forth as she treated a new male patient. She looked right through me. No longer her pal, not the poster girl for recovery.

I hung in there until December when Dr. Z. decided I could stop. No more crutches. I graduated to my cane.

I should have been celebrating the end of PT that final night, but for months I had sat in PT, stricken. Sickened. Embarrassed for I did not know what. Questioning my worth again. I loved my new friends, who now had vanished. Later though, remembering how I had wanted a normal life, I realized I'd had been given one. A life with ups and downs. A realistic life, not perfect, yet normal. I wanted adventure, unpredictable jaunts, staying out late, new people, shady restaurants. I wanted an adolescence. And I had been given one in every way. Looking back, even the way Kate got rid of me seemed perfect and normal. That's how adolescents ditch a friend. One is done. Or wants a cooler friend. I had been participating in my first adolescence.

It took months but finally I felt alive, strong, joyful, brave. Sometimes not totally brave, but I had passed the "test" of 'can she survive social disappointments and betrayals'?

I became more at peace with my religious changes. I had seen others suffering in PT and didn't feel so alone. My feeling of immense gratitude for the surgery remained, even with the long recuperation. I had learned which friends are for keeps and which are blips on the screen.

In other words, I'd finally been living my longed-for "normal" life. Not closed up in my room. Not afraid to take chances.

I'd just experienced my first adventures in adolescence and survived.

LIVING WITH A BREATHING SOUL

I rearranged my house immediately after my PT debacle. Inanimate objects are so easy to handle and they never abandon us.

I moved my twin bed that I still slept in out of my master bedroom and into the guest room. It matched my mom's maple childhood bed on the left side of the room. It had the same headboard with carved turrets on each side.

Now the sun-drenched room had symmetry. I still owned two aqua Indian block print throws from college I used as bedspreads. I placed my green stained-glass lamp on the dresser, perfect for reading by that gentle light. I found new manila rice paper shades at Pier 1 and painted the room a light yellow. I cleaned out the closet ready for someone else's apparel. The room was ready for guests, breathing creatures. Finally I was considering the possibility.

Sue and Jeff offered me a double bed frame. They didn't need it and it was headed to recycling. I drove up to NH and Jeff and I pushed the black iron components into my car. The next day I bought a mattress. The salesman stuffed the plastic wrapped monster into the back of my hatchback, back seats down, rear hatch opened. A new phase. Perhaps ready to leave the "crib" for my "big girl bed."

I opened my mind to the possibility, however foreign, that someday someone might lie in bed with me. The idea didn't feel as terrifying as it had for more than three decades. Of course no one was in the offing, so fearlessness reigned.

David drove up from Medfield and helped me put the bed together and lift the mattress out of the car and up the steep staircase to the second floor. "Don't overdo," he chided.

"I'm fine," I reassured, clomping around in my braces for extra support this working weekend.

After he left for home, I rearranged my bookshelves, donating a portion of my prized high school English books. Out with the old. Now I wish I still had my old copy of *Beowulf* and *King Lear.* Not to mention all my Thomas Hardy novels and plays by Lillian Hellman. I'd love to see what I underlined in high school.

And what to do with all my Christian Science books? Biographies, dictionaries, textbooks, notebooks, concordances, pamphlets, hymnals. Not quite ready to delete all those years of earnest study. From early childhood to now, my collection probably numbered 40. I boxed them up and pushed them into the back of my bedroom closet. The titles were no longer staring at me, making me feel guilty.

I pulled out the beautiful blue and white quilt I bought the weekend after my mom died. I'd been impelled to buy something beautiful that death weekend, nine years before. I had kept the quilt safely wrapped in tissue in my hall closet. The quilt had to be blue, my mom's favorite color. The design is called "the wedding ring." A bit ironic since my parents' marriage was now permanently shattered and God knows there was no wedding in my offing.

But the quilt called to me with its circular flow and two-tone blue fabric so intricate in design and precise in its handstitched execution. A labor of love by some Amish seamstress. It seemed perfect for wrapping myself up in a comforting hug. But once I got it home all those years ago, it had seemed too beautiful to use. And it hadn't made me feel better at all, unlike most of my retail therapy expeditions. Now though, a voice came to me, *Enjoy it. It's a blanket, not a shroud.* So I unfurled it across the bed.

Later in the day I sorted out clothes that made me feel too young. I tossed anything with tempera paint and permanent marker stains. I don't have to JUST be a teacher.

I donated a cardigan of my mom's that I had kept for so long. I put Mom's picture in a tiny brass heart frame, one of the few I had before her cancer, on my dresser. If I cried, I cried. I decided I'd try to look at her picture instead of staring at her blue Nordic sweater that she wore until it hung on her bones. Her favorite piece of clothing from a trip she and Dad had taken to Switzerland decades before. A business trip for Dad, but a vacation for Mom. She even got to see her aunt and cousin, Jurgin, in Wuppertal, Germany, her ancestors' hometown.

I allowed myself to consider happier times. How Mom and I loved lobster. We'd drive to Cape Cod in the fall just to have it one last time before winter. We'd stop at the Chatham light house and watch the wind whip the waves into whitecaps. In December we'd wrap Christmas gifts for Dad together on Christmas Eve. Those times seemed so long ago. But that picture in the heart frame was proof she once had a blemish-free smile. I kept taking that blue sweater in and out of the donation bag in the corner of my room. I fought the sense of giving away a piece of her. It wasn't easy driving away from that Goodwill bin next to the grocery store.

Days later, I added some hangers to my downstairs coat closet, in case someone dropped in unexpectedly. Maybe I'd become the hospitable hostess. In the past, I'd usually made sure my front door was locked and the security chain latched. Curtains always closed, so I could pretend I wasn't home if need be. Even if my car sat parked in the driveway, I'd often hide and not answer the doorbell.

Hard to admit I was still isolating at 38.

I remember one summer evening a few years before my surgery, three school friends came to my door at around 9 pm the day school got out. They had invited me to dinner, but I had said no. So they came by after dinner and sang out, "Peggy, we know you're in there. Don't pretend you're not. We see you hiding in there" (which they couldn't). The quasi-humorous threats made me open the door. They tried to convince me to go with them up to Hampton Beach, but I stood behind the locked screen door while they told me their idea. I didn't invite them in. Our gym teacher, whom we all loved, was working a summer police beat up on the waterfront. They wanted to go up and say "hi" to him. My mind was not yet in the "I'll do anything" mode or "fun is okay."

But looking back, I think of the loyalty of these school friends, Sherry, Terry, and Sue Ellis. They never gave up on me.

The last object I needed for my new life might be considered an impulse buy. Kind of a big-ticket item. I felt sure I deserved it, having survived surgery, months of recuperation, and PT. So off I went to Lechmere Sales, the Best Buy of the 1980s. I bought myself an ultra-modern stereo system that played records, radio, CDs, and tapes. Two humungous speakers for each end of the couch were a bit overpowering in my tiny living room, but I needed loud music if I was going to begin my longed-for social life. I'd used music to drown out my fears before. I needed these trappings to ease into my new outgoing persona.

Not too great at mechanical or electrical set-ups, I surprised myself by calling Joe. Joe attended the Christian Science church. He was about my age, but not a "lifer" like me. Our mutual friends Mark and Beth had brought him into the religion at about age 30, when he was healed of alcoholism.

Friends at church were sure we'd be a match. But Joe and I didn't click, and there was too much pressure. He was even more shy than I was. However, we were friends with the pressure off. I knew him as an amazing computer and electronics geek as well. I got up the nerve to call him, and he came right over, unloaded my car, and set up the pieces in no time. We sat on the floor blasting Michael Bolton CDs. The living room floor vibrated to the powerful base setting. Perfect.

I told him I owed him a pizza. Looking back I was getting quite gutsy asking others for help.

Was I ready to cohabitate with a breathing soul yet?

Sue called and reported that Basil had just delivered 12 black lab/German shepherd pups. She told me the story of the teensy runt, not breathing at birth. How Jeff took the limp body and did mouth to mouth and heart massage with this pup wrapped in an old beach towel. Miraculously this miniscule female pup survived. She asked me if I wanted to come up that weekend and take a look.

This loomed as yet another test. As a dog person growing up, I'd get so attached that I'd fall apart when one of the dogs died or was rehomed, usually when I was at camp. Our family had horrible luck with dogs. Our beloved sheltie, Kilty, was mauled to death by a boxer, while my dad was on a business trip. When I was 8, my schnauzer, Heidi, had kidney problems and died after just two years. My dad gave a "destructive" German shepherd puppy away after she destroyed several houseplants while we were at church. And our last sheltie, scared of men, hid unless my dad wore his bathrobe. So the terrified puppy was sent back to the breeder. No replacement, just a refund.

Our last dog, my mom's schnauzer Penny, sat loyally with Mom until she left for hospice. My dad couldn't stand Penny's presence with

Mom gone, so one Saturday, he coerced my brother and his wife to drive poor Penny to Angell Memorial and had her put to sleep.

These losses stayed with me. I treasured their dog tags, collars, and pictures. Between our list of past dog losses and the loss of my mom, I didn't know if I had the emotional fortitude for a puppy.

I drove up to Sue's house that weekend. There, in the living room, in a whelping box Jeff had built, were the 12 tiny pups, eyes not yet open. Little baby sounds and grunts coming out of the box. The pups, the size of hotdog buns.

True, I had an equal fear of commitment and death. But stronger was my absolute passion for babies. Human babies, puppies, gerbils, guppies. Kittens, too, if I hadn't been allergic.

Jeff held the little runt. An adorable black little creature with white paws and a tiny white chest. The smallest tail ever. I already had a name for "my" puppy, so I'm pretty sure the dog's destiny was sealed even before I drove up. Her story spoke to me. She was a survivor.

I named her Dorsi, short for dorsiflexion, an amazing skill I had, now that I had heels and straight feet. Dorsi could be my live-in pal.

Dorsi came home eight weeks later. She cried and yelped the entire hour ride home to Newburyport. I stopped in a McDonald's parking lot to try to comfort her. But the stopping of the car made her shake and gag. I started singing my memorized Christian Science hymns to her.

Fear grabbed me. See, I'm not a natural mother. And what's with the gagging?

This commitment thing, a shocker, a time suck, a worry. Can I keep such a small animal alive? I kept myriad gerbils, a rabbit, a red slider turtle named Tootsie, and a huge cichlid fish family alive in my classroom. But ownership, right in my home, seemed much more personal and intense. I willed myself to bond because in the back of my mind, if I could handle having Dorsi in the house, perhaps someday I could "stand" to have a baby. Not "stand," like tolerate an odious experience but stand to feel the deep love and commitment I'd felt for my mom. I'd need to tolerate inevitable loss again with the ultimate living creature, a child. A child that had to grow up eventually and leave home. Leave me.

A life-long dream of adoption rushed back. It could happen with or without a partner. Just like buying a house. Now that I could walk straight and wasn't as morose, perhaps at some point I could pass an adoption agency home study. Since my self-loathing seemed to be dissipating, I thought possibly I'd qualify in the future as an adoptive mother. I wanted to instill joy, love, possibilities. My main priority: not to totally screw a kid up and cause permanent harm. So I started with Dorsi, my test case.

This black fur ball cried all night until I put a sleeping bag next to her crate. I slept there, with my finger stuck in the crate for her to lick, for two weeks. Out of the crate one morning, she thanked me by shredding the corner of the new sleeping bag with her razor sharp teeth. I kind of treasure that sleeping bag's ripped lining now that Dorsi's gone. She died at 14.

In her puppyhood, Dorsi flung herself in her water dish in the kitchen and splashed like it was a wading pool. Always in a good mood, just for fun, one day, she ate a chunk of the burgundy oriental rug I had inherited from my grandparents. Tassels and triangular chunk now missing after clearing the gate in the kitchen and landing on the rug in the dining room. She seemed very contrite as I banished her to the deck. She cried by the back door, while I cried inside and rolled up the damaged rug. Heirlooms do not cohabitate well with baby living creatures, who are teething. She gifted me with several piles of throw-up to prove she was the culprit.

Dorsi woke up at all hours of the night whimpering. In an effort to housebreak her, I carried her on my shoulder multiple times down the steps and outside to pee. This must be how it feels to change a diaper in the middle of the night. During the day she howled if she couldn't see me. For a small puppy, her bark seemed to ricochet off the walls. I started to get worried about going back to school in the fall. Eight hours alone is a long day for a puppy.

Dorsi's big brown eyes almost made up for my consternation that she was running, and sometimes ruining, my summer. In my mature moments, she seemed the sweetest little thing. Like an Oreo cookie with big ears. Luckily my neighbors were dog people. Chris offered to come in each day at noon to let Dorsi out when I went back to school. I tried placing her crate as far away from that shared wall as possible. Finally, I fenced off my yard, with a wooden gate that locked. Eventually she stayed outside when I was at school. The cozy plastic igloo doghouse in case of rain eased my guilt.

For sure, Dorsi tied me down. I had just begun to consider having fun in my life and now this. I called Sue, who told me it would get easier. Lots of exercise, she said, lots of obedience school. I always followed Sue's advice, my role model for common sense.

I also needed to ponder and get perspective regarding putting someone else first again. I had put my mom first when she was ill. I had needed to put myself first while I was recovering. I had to remember I *chose* Dorsi. She was not a "have to." I needed to look at her puppyhood as *fun*. I needed to lighten up and not take her every move so seriously. Dorsi never really came to the understanding that I was the alpha in the house. She was having the time of her life. I think she considered me just along for the ride.

I met people walking her. "She looks like such a happy puppy," they commented. *That's worth something,* I thought. After all, she wasn't a student who needs to march to the beat and meet curriculum guidelines.

I took my girl to obedience class, where I didn't hide but joined in all the activities. Dorsi thought those classes were one big play date. Not a serious bone in her sleek body. She had become a lanky, uncoordinated, goofball. I learned later that black labs are like that. Dorsi never rose to star student of the obedience class.

I introduced her to Plum Island, the best beach ever. She plopped down and refused to move. Eventually she got used to "her" beach. She ran, I watched. She had the best dorsiflexion I'd ever seen.

Somehow, she knew I needed a little softening up. Each day when I'd drive up the driveway from school, she'd be sitting on top of the picnic table on the deck, at attention, waiting for me. She'd jump off the table, tail whipping around, as I opened the gate.

I got attached to the breathing in the house. Dorsi and I became family.

SANDY POINT SYNCHRONICITY

Sandy Point Beach, October 1990.

The eight-mile unpaved ride down the reservation road keeps me bumping up and down in the driver's seat. Crunching pebbles fly to either side of the front tires. The marsh on the right sparkles in the October early-morning light. Birds in small flocks are flitting back and forth to my left. The grasses are swaying, bayberry bushes in full bloom on the sides of the road.

This road leads to my holy sanctuary, Sandy Point Beach.

I back into the narrow handicapped space, tires sinking into the white sand. No Sunday church clothes required, just jeans, a t-shirt, and a hooded sweatshirt to protect from the whipping winds on the point. The tide is on its way in. This day I plan a walk on the beach, no rock hopping, or tide pooling at low tide. I come without Dorsi. I need to think.

I carry a heart-throbbing question. Can I afford to raise a child? A child not yet here. Perhaps a child not even born. Pondering adoption all my life, was I finally in a position to act?

Clubfeet repaired four years ago. Recuperated enough to walk this beach without crutches or cane. Snazzy turquoise sneakers. I trek along the edge of the water, hands in fuzzy sweatshirt pockets.

Firm sand from the absorbed lapping water supports my walking. A golden retriever and his master, only specks, downwind to the left.

Is there an answer here? Who or what can tell me, for sure, what to do? I'm not so much into prayer anymore. I'm relying on nature, my instinct, something different from hymns or Bible verses.

I ponder the twinkling Sunday horizon. I gaze at the gentle waves, covering more sand, leaving a glistening shadow behind. Clustered bubbles of foam. Never-changing rhythms.

Ever-present creatures now hiding under the rocks, hidden by high tide. Reappearing, as always, at low tide. I look down at the rippled patterns in the sand. Mathematical, artistic. Gradually a unique pattern catches my eye. The sand, rising in small circles, surrounds me.

What will it take for me to begin that yearned-for great leap to parenthood?

Listening to my voice, logic says no. Too old at 42. Financially no. Funds sparse after costs not covered by health insurance during my recuperation. Fear says no. Won't be approved. I lack the qualifications. Lack. "Shhhhh," I demand, shaking my head to silence so many negative voices.

I look down again. I lean down and flick at the circular mini-mound of sand.

A purple sand dollar uncovers itself. Alive. I flick next to it, another. I flick all around me. A message. Abundance where lack appears: 65 of them, dampening my sweatshirt pockets.

I go to the edge of the water and gently place the purple fuzzy, so-alive sand dollars back into the salty water. It's common to find a single white-washed one in one piece. No longer alive. I keep those aged sand dollars displayed in a canister on my kitchen counter. But here, this morning, I find 65 alive. Their black hairs gently swaying.

That Sunday morning, that very time, that specific tide, those sand dollars waiting for me, right where I stand. Showing me the unseen can become the seen.

My healing place. I feel it, I see it, and I trust it.

MLK Day

They started arriving at 5 pm.

I moved my car to the lawn, so I'd be able to back the car out and pick up the Chinese food. I hated being blocked in. My sloping driveway fit three cars vertically. The extras parked along the front on the street. Luckily there was no snow expected, so no parking ban.

The idea started in the teacher's room when a bunch of us lamented the limited time to talk together as we gulped down lunch and hustled to the ladies room. We had different schedules, life commitments, etc. Plus, we always just talked school talk during the week. We needed time together to just veg and relax.

Then I remembered MLK Day was coming up in a couple of weeks. "What if we had an old-fashioned sleepover?"

Then out of my mouth came "I have plenty of room at my house. Two couches, two twin beds, plenty of rug space for sleeping bags, too." They jumped at the idea. One friend who couldn't sleep over said she'd bring drinks and come at least for dinner and chatting. The others were up for the whole shebang.

Right then, before leaving the teacher's room, they threw in $10/piece and told me what Chinese food they wanted. I said, no need to chip in, but they laughingly said, "That's what party goers do. You'll learn."

Several friends volunteered wine for the Chinese food, and orange juice and cream cheese for the morning bagels. Sherry, Terry, Liz L., Sue Ellis, Nancy A., and Sue from New Hampshire. Finally I'd get to use my dining room table for more than folding laundry. I pulled out my heavy Pfaltzgraff plates that I never got to use, usually eating off paper plates when I ate alone. I'd get to use my idle dishwasher as well.

Planning for that Monday in January made the week before go by fast. Plus it was something to look forward to over the weekend, besides lesson plans and Dorsi and our weekend beach visit.

The gang straggled in with pillows, blankets, and grocery bags. I learned how party-goers often bring something to share and then something else too. Not just wine, they added cheese and crackers. Not just orange juice, but muffins, too. Not just soda, but lots of chips, salsa, and pretzels. It felt like Christmas. Lots of laughter and relaxation. Then around 8 pm, I made the Chinese restaurant take-out run. Two brown bags with enough food for many more than the seven of us.

My first sleepover at 40 and hosting the event. This would have made my mom happy. We talked in our pajamas and bathrobes till way past midnight. Dorsi ate up the attention and loved seeing her first human, Sue Harbour.

Finally we were talked out and we staked our claims to beds, couches, and space on the floor. The house seemed happy being fully occupied. I didn't turn the heat down, making sure everyone was toasty on this freezing January night.

I got up early. Dorsi and I tiptoed downstairs to let her out. I had this childlike joy at seeing my friends sleeping, spread out in the living room. The ease I felt that morning gave me confidence, delight, and a sparkly sense of energy. Being with people you love is not scary at all.

And yes, they left by midmorning.

That fear of being invaded blew out the door. The event became a tradition, well, a two-year tradition.

The second yearly MLK sleep over, I added a friend Sherry introduced me to. She seemed like she'd fit in well, even though she wasn't a teacher.

She stayed when the rest of them left, midmorning.

We went for a long walk with Dorsi at Maudsley State Park. The snow-covered pines and paths seemed magical that Monday afternoon. The sun beat down, with shadows and sparkles. This new person adored Dorsi.

She was the first one I told that I had a home study by an adoption agency scheduled for early February. She thought adoption sounded fabulous.

That day was the beginning of a sacred building journey, a journey to "family." Not a traditional one, but one nonetheless. It seemed safe with Carol. Right then, having someone besides Dorsi walking with me didn't seem claustrophobic at all. My family expanded: Carol, Dorsi, and me.

PART VI

THE MOTHER

BABY JENNA

The Air China plane touched down on June 8ᵗʰ, in Wuhan. This was definitely not an airport, but a military base. No one had warned us about this unusual arrival, which turned out to be just the first of many unexpected circumstances we'd encounter and learn to accept without blinking. The dripping wet air wrapped itself around us. Our clothes and bodies were immediately drenched as the plane door opened. Sweat dripped off my forehead onto my passport I gripped. Over the next month the stifling temperature and humidity never budged.

We exited the plane on metal stairs down to the boiling black tarmac. I could feel the intense heat through my sneakers. Palm trees dotted the cracked soil off in the distance. To the side of the staircase, I glimpsed a uniformed soldier behind a bush holding a rifle aimed at the plane. "Look over there," I whispered to Carol.

"Yikes," she whispered back.

The passengers from the jet silently filed into a cement room, filled with cigarette smoke. The plane had been full. But the domestic passengers vaporized quickly. No need for them to show their passports. Perhaps their luggage occupied another room. Maybe we were so preoccupied by this numbing scene that we didn't notice them pass us by.

A soldier, in green Mao military garb was standing behind a podium. The four of us, American women, were directed to stand in line behind the podium, passports opened to the visa page. No smile or welcome. We stood silently.

My eyes darted to Caitlyn, Renee, and Carol. We each had the same flat affect. That affect of, *okay, we can do this. Now it begins. No one do anything stupid.* I knew Carol, but had only met the other two adoptive moms two days before in Hong Kong. I had no idea yet how they'd hold it together.

Renee seemed cool, almost cold, and privileged. She looked as if she should fly first class. Her black business suit and coiffed hair and nails made a statement, at least to me. Sophisticated. It would take a baby with a big ego to handle Renee.

Caitlyn looked very fragile, as if this was the first day of school and she was petrified to leave her mother. She giggled a lot, but not from humor, kind of like on the verge of hysteria. I could sense her tender heart right away as her eyes glazed over, tears brimming as we maneuvered through this unusual travel day. She had a husband, Steve, back home in Massachusetts. That's all I knew about her at that moment. Later I learned she had two young sons at home. No wonder she looked on the verge of tears. She'd be away from them for a month. The social worker had told her not to let on about her children.

China wanted these first adopted girls to be only children when they arrived to their new homes. Very ironic how the one child policy favored boys, but China wanted us to favor their girls. These tiny girls should be the center of attention in their new homes. We were only too happy to oblige.

There was no English spoken at this make shift airport. The soldier stamped our passports forcefully. Now besides the fog of smoke in the room, it smelled moldy, and felt exceedingly damp. We'd soon discover this assault on the senses was a major part of our China experience.

We entered a larger barren room, and right in the middle we eyed our luggage, heaped in a pile. A wide-eyed, rosy cheeked, teenager stood next to our belongings. He wore blue shorts, a white polo shirt tucked in and plastic sandals. He had a short-cropped haircut, and weighed less than 100 lbs. and around 5'4." He looked like an elementary school boy, maybe 10. It turned out he was a teenager, 14 years old.

"Peggy?" "Renee?" "Caitlyn?" The voice belonged to that kid standing next to our luggage. I introduced him to Carol, the fourth American staring at him. He spoke perfect English. His name was Shu Hui. His mother, a pediatric nurse at the local Wuhan University hospital sometimes helped ill children at the Wuhan Orphanage. Shu Hui, Min Hua, his mom, and Shu Hui's dad, a chemistry professor at Wuhan University, lived down the hill from where we'd be staying. "I'm your neighbor," Shu Hui declared. This teenager had been given the job by the orphanage to "fetch" us with an orphanage driver. They drove in an old, stripped down rusty ambulance used by the orphanage for multiple tasks.

We each had two oversized duffel bags. The adoption agency advised us to bring enough diapers, wipes, clothes, baby medicine and formula for the entire month. Diapers were not used in the 90s in China. Babies wore split pants, and were held over a curb or bucket to pee and poop on command. Clothes, medicine and formula could be obtained in the inner city shopping district of Wuhan, but we'd be isolated in a college guesthouse on the edge of the city.

Medicine was doled out at Chinese hospitals, not pharmacies, if seriously ill. Not a week or a month's worth like home, but one dose at a time, in person at the hospital. Wuhan University Hospital was about a 15-minute walk from our guesthouse. But the rumor mill had told us not to take our babies to a Chinese hospital unless they were in dire shape. IVs were injected in their heads, was the scary hearsay. Usually herbal remedies were used on Chinese babies mixed in their homes, if they were moderately under the weather. I brought one small bottle of Pediacare. I'd never given medicine to a baby. If I had known better, I'd have brought several more bottles of meds. Then again giving meds to a baby you've just met is a daunting thought. How much is enough? Are they allergic to anything?

Shu Hui and the driver hoisted our bags into the back of the ambulance. We climbed in and sat on plastic milk crates. The small front and side windows were open to let in any existing breeze. A chairman Mao plastic red medallion hung on the mirror up front.

The ambulance pulled out of the base. For the first time we heard the distinct shrill honking of Chinese vehicles as we bumped along the potholed road. We sat solemnly, dazed, and shell shocked. What a change from modern, glitzy Hong Kong, where we had spent our first two days to this no man's land. Shu Hui turned around in the passenger seat and asked, "The flight was good?" We were polite Americans on our best behavior. "Oh yes, very good."

We were still jet lagged from the 12-hour time change. I felt tipped upside down, and slightly dizzy, not to mention petrified at what my dream of motherhood had morphed into thus far. Endless hours of flying, and a city of over eight million, shockingly poor. It's one thing to read and hear about poverty, another to be in its presence. I was on high alert watching the run down cement tenements on the outskirts of the city pass me by.

We passed yellow taxis careening in and out, and around each other with no lane markings. They barely missed hitting stray dogs that sauntered on the sidewalks and streets. The bored looking drivers had cigarettes hanging from their lips.

There were huge billboards on the sides of the road with Chinese parents and one baby boy. We understood the meaning of those posters immediately without deciphering the Chinese characters. That's why we were here. That one child depicted on the poster told it all.

The other vehicles on the road were official military olive green boxy cars and pick-up trucks. Soldiers hung over the sides of the truck for some air. The soldiers eyed us from their much taller vehicles. The military vehicles and taxis seemed to beep their horns for no reason. I started saying hymns to myself, to calm myself from this visual overload.

We noticed bikes loaded with watermelons in baskets, young children, arms around the waist of a parent, balancing perfectly. They rode along the side of the roads. Vendors, on the sidewalks sold single bottles of unrefrigerated coke from a crate, or mended old shoes and flat bicycle tires. We paused at stop signs to let the pedestrians cross. They looked exhausted and dusty as they squinted at us in our vehicle. It was uncommon to see Caucasian faces in Wuhan in 1992. It's never been a tourist spot for westerners. In those days only, Shanghai, Beijing, Guangzhou and Hong Kong drew tourists.

We passed red, white and blue tattered plastic awnings with men sleeping under them, children squatting to pee, and women, holding umbrellas, sitting on plastic three-legged stools out of the blistering sun.

Shu Hui told us we were getting closer. He said we'd be staying at Wuhan University, "very famous university." There was no room at the foreign guesthouse on campus. There was only one hotel in Wuhan that allowed western tourists in those days, he remarked, and that was full.

We'd be staying at the domestic guesthouse at the university. Already a group from another adoption agency was in the foreign guesthouse. They received their babies yesterday, Shu Hui remarked. Our ears perked up. "How are they?" we asked. "Some are very sick, very thin," Shu Hui reported. "My mother is checking on them every day. Two have fevers." I wanted to bite my lip at the description of the ill babies. I told myself to stay calm and not assume the worst, a hard habit of mine to break.

The ambulance wound up a steep hill. I could make out brick and white concrete buildings in the hazy distance. Lush bushes, trees and red flowers lined the driveway, as we got closer. Male students played ping-pong outside on concrete ping-pong tables. We wound around and went higher still. The Chinese flag drooped in the sultry air outside of the domestic guesthouse.

Shu Hui motioned the driver to stop. The domestic guesthouse looked like a cement college dorm. Non-descript. Shu Hui reported the elevator was broken. "You're all on the fourth floor. I'll pick you up later for dinner and take you to my mother's." Oh, how sweet, I thought. He'll pick us up. He must know how tired we are. Then he asked outright, with his broad innocent smile, "Do you have any American money?"

Actually we had wads of American money in our money belts next to our sweaty waists. The adoption fee of $3,000 in those days was brought in crisp brand new 100-dollar bills. We also had extra American cash for "emergencies," which could have been interpreted as bribe money. I preferred to think of the money as tip money. We had heard, though, that one of the mothers-to-be in the foreign guesthouse had bought the orphanage a washing machine before she came to China. I don't know if she thought she'd get a healthier baby that way but the whole concept seemed in poor taste. I was so innocent in the 90s.

So, us four sweaty, exhausted Americans stood stunned by Shu Hui's request for American money. I think it didn't register in our jetlagged brains that he hoped for a tip. We soon learned that American currency was prized. It was worth more than Chinese currency. The best gift you could give a Chinese citizen in those days was American cash.

We dragged our overstuffed duffels into the lobby. Shu Hui left for his home on foot.

A gentleman at the reception desk, who only spoke Chinese, looked at us suspiciously and brought us up to our rooms. He motioned to leave the luggage downstairs for now. He must have wanted to show us our rooms before his shift ended. We climbed the four flights up the marble stairs.

It was stifling hot in the hall, as I cautiously opened the door to our new home. It was the last brown metal door on the right. Across from the door a porthole-shaped window gave us the sight of the city of Wuhan off in the hazy distance. He showed us the door down the hall to the rooftop where we could hang wet clothes that we'd be washing by hand. God, it was brutal up there. The black tar roof sizzled.

We female adoptive parents were the only ones on this floor. Chinese students studying for the summer were housed on the first and second floor. The third floor housed the cafeteria.

Our room, #410, had cement walls with filthy green carpet. The bathroom needed a good scrubbing, but we were told to bring Ajax and I did. There were open, sliding windows on one side of the bedroom. A garbagy smell wafted up, and there were no screens on the windows. We immediately learned about the famous gargantuan Wuhan mosquitos. Welts as big as fifty-cent pieces dotted our thighs and arms within minutes. No one at our agency had told us to bring mosquito netting. Too late now.

We heard military marching music playing from loudspeakers somewhere close by. Every hour on the hour, during the day, a military song blared. It might have been China's national anthem. I kept thinking of American tv news shows I'd seen with thousands of Chinese soldiers marching in tandem, heads to the left, rifles over their shoulders. I hoped it was just a music recording coming from some loud speaker, not a real military base nearby.

Out the window, down below was a compost pile of rotting food. Roaming chickens pecked at food remnants. We were told by the adoption agency that our rooms were air-conditioned. But that was at the foreign guesthouse, not ours. In Chinese travel books Wuhan is dubbed, the "furnace of the Yangtze." So it was close the windows and sweat, or open and be eaten by mosquitos. We opted for the mosquitos.

We hustled back downstairs and began hauling up our luggage. No one dared complain yet. We all smiled desperate, stoic smiles. *One day at a time,* I kept telling myself. The adoption agency had met with us before we left and urged us to be on our best behavior. This was a new program. *Don't ruin it for others,* the agency implored. Americans have a reputation for being demanding, we were told at our last meeting. So we smiled, nodded, and acted unfazed by our new surroundings.

Luckily Carol and I were campers. We camped on weekends in Maine or New Hampshire as part of getting to know each other. We both loved the outdoors and adventures. We were used to fetching water, making a fire, hauling equipment to set up. Outhouses, and unpredictable weather conditions were the norm. Before we left for China we'd visited REI sporting store, to get some freeze dried food, and sweat wicking t-shirts for the trip. I eyed a Eureka 4-person tent set up in the store. I told Carol, jokingly; if we came back alive I was treating myself to that tent.

We'd need to be campers to survive this Chinese adventure.

Carol lugged up my luggage and hers to our guesthouse room, taking many sweaty trips. Carol had offered to be my "sherpa" on this trip. She knew the history of my feet, and we plotted out how I could keep walking and doing what I needed to do for a month without making it obvious that I had limitations in walking. She did the heavy lifting. She scouted out the easiest way to get from point A to B. This is a job Carol loved and still loves. It allows her to be independent, yet needed. She is our family's scout. Always reporting back.

We became an excellent team during this time. When I thought I couldn't go one more step, she'd encourage, *"We've got this."* When she was afraid we'd never get back home, and her snazzy camera actually stopped functioning because of the heat, I encouraged, *"You are doing so well. Remember how you like adventures? You can use my point and click camera."*

I began Ajaxing every surface, tub, sink, toilet and counters. We started to set up shop when someone came in and motioned to us to go to the cafeteria with our money. I cannot remember how we understood this command, but Carol and the others followed. The cafeteria didn't mind that we only had American dollars, all the better. We pre-paid for 30 days of meals.

I remember being amazed that we were only charged $3 a day per person. During our stay the kitchen staff provided us with tea, water, hot rice cereal, and steamed buns for breakfast. Lunch was rice and some chicken or fish dish, and green vegetables. The vegetables in the summer were fresh, and we named our favorite green beans, "Wuhan beans." For dinner there was rice again, vegetables, and some kind of stir-fry. The meat in the stir-fry was sometimes hard to identify, except for the one dinner when a platter of cooked frogs came out in a symmetrical circle on a platter. We left those poor frogs untouched.

Our assigned seats were in an enclosed glass dining room. The drapes were closed. They wanted us isolated from any students or visitors. No hobnobbing in those days. So at mealtimes the four of us sat together at a big round table, clumsily taking food from a lazy Susan with chopsticks. This room was air-conditioned which was an exciting discovery. Any cool breeze was a gift in Wuhan.

The manager of the guesthouse pointed out a furnace room on our floor where there was a hot water spigot, with boiling water. We each had a tall metal thermos in our rooms. This boiled water was pure for mixing baby formula. Carol took on that job each day of filling the thermos with water for bottles once Jenna arrived. Each day I scoured with my Ajax, and hand washed our clothes. We brought rope and duct tape to set up a drying line across the bedroom. We didn't need our underwear blowing in the breeze on the rooftop.

I spotted one brown phone on a desk in the hall, but it had no dials on it and no dial tone. There were no cell phones yet. With no interpreter in the guesthouse and no working phone, we couldn't call home, until we got to Guangzhou three weeks out, where we'd receive the babies' visas to go to America. My heart sank at that one, but I had no time to dwell on the isolation. The barrage of new information kept us moving automatically.

The four of us hadn't figured out how we'd know when Shu Hui returned to take us to dinner that first night. This was the first of many times, where random people involved with the orphanage showed up, motioned for us to come, and we followed. The adoption program in Wuhan had only opened eight months before. It had two other families up to now. There was no "usual" to depend on.

Changsha was the other city allowing American adoptions. That program was opened only for married couples. It was supposed to be less primitive, as those parents stayed in a hotel. Decades later hundreds of cities were open for adoptions. Not only did the expansion of the adoption program meet the need for the abandoned orphans, but the money funneled in by the adoption fees, called donations, helped modernize the orphanages. Eventually in the summer there was air conditioning, and in the winter, heat. The fees also provided washing machines and dryers, and updated vans.

Water from the tap in our bathroom was not "potable." I draped a washcloth on the faucet to remind myself. Carol had seen water bottles for sale in the cafeteria during the tour, so went and brought back as many as she could hold.

There wasn't a crib, so I pushed the two twin beds together and put a quilt from one of them going down the center for a safe place for Jenna to sleep.

I had a 4-ounce and an 8-ounce Playtex bottle with enlarged holes in the nipples, which we cut with scissors before leaving for the trip. The adoption agency told us the holes needed to be larger, because the babies were used to fast feedings, with so many infants in the orphanage. I put out a can of the soy-powdered formula next to the diapers. Chinese babies do not drink cow's milk. Soy is the protein (tofu) and drink of preference.

As I leaned out the window with no screens, Renee was looking out her window in disgust and we caught each other's eye. She looked totally mortified at the compost heap below, not to mention the free-range chickens.

All I could think to say to her was, "Remember why we are here."

Shu Hui appeared to take us to his mom's and dad's. I then realized that "picking you up" in China meant, coming by foot to lead you down the right streets or paths to the destination.

Half set up, we followed him out the double doors of our dorm, and left the campus.

We followed Shu Hui down a winding driveway, to a staircase with beautiful peonies on either side. Their apartment building of whitewashed cement, contrasted with a red tile roof. Leafed trees shielded the building from the blistering heat of the late afternoon sun.

We entered and walked up two flights of cement stairs. We passed the community toilet and kitchen that was out in a hallway for all to share. Then we entered a room with two beds, with red, silk bedspreads. A calendar was taped to the wall, and a framed picture of ancestors sat on the top of the piano. The piano and bench took up the other wall. We met Min Hua, Shu Hui's mom and the orphanage nurse, and her husband. Only Shu Hui spoke English, but we knew "Ni Hao," which meant "Hello, "and smiled nervously. Shu Hui's father welcomed us with his sweet smile.

We sat on folding chairs around a square card table, set up in the middle of their living room. Then, like clockwork plate after plate of delicacy was piled on that table. All seven of us sat down and ate this meal Min Hua had cooked for our welcome. Dumplings, seaweed salad, Ma Po tofu, bok choy, tomatoes, eggs, noodles w/ little mini shrimps, pork ribs, fruit and sweet candy. A banquet is 12 dishes in China, and we had all 12. Some exploded in my mouth with spiciness. Luckily there was a liter of warm Coke in the middle of the table, too. So I took gulps of that from my glass when my mouth ignited.

His parents were so proud of Shu Hui, their only child. They told him to play the piano for us. His parents clapped and we joined in with applause. "A good student," Min Hua said, "very smart. Maybe come to America someday for college." It seemed the more time we spent in China, the more we learned about the dream parents had for their only child to study in America.

To have a nurse so close to our guesthouse, and Shu Hui's English proficiency not to mention his positive attitude, gave the four of us comfort as we trudged back up the hill after dinner. This time we knew to tip Shu Hui with those crisp dollar bills.

As we entered the lobby, Sunshine, an interpreter hired by the orphanage, greeted us. She had a Chinese name, but took on Sunshine because she told us we'd be able to pronounce it.

She reported in the morning she'd meet us in the lobby and we'd go into the city to the Provincial bureau that needed to record our adoption paperwork. Everything in China needs a red stamp of approval. This was our first step in finalizing the adoptions, so we could "receive" the babies.

Sunshine told Carol she'd need to wait back at the guesthouse, as the taxi would only have room for her in the front, and Caitlyn, Renee, and I in the back. She reminded us again and again to bring all our paperwork. Before we left for China, our packets of 15 adoption documents had been translated into Chinese, authenticated in our state house in Boston, and notarized to prove their authenticity in New York City.

Finally Carol would have some alone time to explore. She loves poking around in a new area, and somehow had the ability to make friends with or without the native language. She prepared her backpack, sunscreen and straw hat for the next day.

Before bed, she and I discussed how it would be great if she could find the foreign guesthouse so we could meet some of the adoptive parents that already had their children. If we knew were the foreign guesthouse was, Carol and I could take a walk there after dinner to introduce ourselves. Just to have a feeling for how sick or needy their infants were would calm my mind and give me a sense of the reality to come. The shock of a new home, mother, food, and language, must certainly take a toll on any baby.

Loving a quest, Carol went to bed happy that a smidge of independence was still hers.

Meanwhile the mosquitos buzzed.

June 10th, 1992.

The day is hazy and humid as usual. We are still jet -lagged but gaining our footing in Wuhan, China. We awkwardly grasp chopsticks and eat dumplings and vegetables for breakfast. Todd hears we might go to the bank in the city today. Todd, an adoptive father, who arrived a few days after our group, always seems to have information we do not. He perseverates at each meal that we must measure the circumference of each baby's head to make sure it is normal. We stare at him. I am not going to whip out a tape measure when I'm handed my baby.

Sunshine, the interpreter who appears when there are official tasks to accomplish, runs in and says we are going into the city immediately. We need to get Chinese money. The bus is waiting. We rush back to our rooms to retrieve our backpacks. The ancient bus clatters down the Wuhan University hill.

We drive over the bridge into a busy area of the city. We're told that there are three parts to this huge "furnace of the Yangtze,"

Wuchang, Hanko, and Hanyang. The Yellow Crane Tower looms on the right. We don't imagine we'll do any sightseeing.

The bus stops but leaves its motor running.

Sunshine leads us into a great white marble building. Local customers stare at us in the cavernous bank. It was built by the British in World War II. The military guards have rifles drawn. Our voices echo as we ask what line to stand in. Thank God Sunshine accompanies us. It is a plum job for a college student. When we leave China with our babies, she'll receive generous tips. She'll have grateful contacts in the US if she wants to study stateside, a Chinese student's dream in the 90s. Sunshine radiates enthusiasm and knowledge.

Renee asks if we will see the orphanage today since we finished the adoption paperwork yesterday at the Civil Affairs Bureau. We have no idea what our babies look like yet. No pictures accompany the "referrals" to prospective parents in 1992. We can hardly wait to see them in person.

Sunshine says our banking is taking too long and now there is no time. Translations are confusing. We accept any decree. We have no itinerary. We get back on the sweltering bus. We must be going back to the university, I think. But all of us brought baby supplies and gifts in our backpacks just in case. I am totally disoriented and just breathe down my t-shirt to stay cool. We turn off onto a dirt side street.

All of a sudden Sunshine says, "This is the road to the orphanage." "We are going to the orphanage?" Caitlyn asks. "Yes, and we will get your babies and have lunch."

A historic event cannot occur without a meal. In China it is the rule of hospitality. Their traditional greeting in Chinese is, "Have you eaten?"

We look at each other in shock. Plans change so fast in China. It keeps us untethered, off balance, as events spring up unexpectedly. I stare out the window trying to memorize the narrow alley with vendors all along the side of the road. I want to come back to this street since it's close to the orphanage. Maybe Jenna's parents are in the crowd shopping today. Cooked chickens hang from wires in the sizzling hot sun. Pig hides are next to them. String beans and watermelon overflow the stands. Suntanned vendors stare at us in the bus as we stop and go to avoid hitting crossing pedestrians. The orphanage bus beeps its sharp horn. When I hear it, I am still stunned, "I am in China, I am in China."

My heart is bursting.

The bus stops at a gazebo with overflowing geraniums. The building ahead looks like a Spanish hacienda. Three nurses in uniforms are standing in the gateway holding dark-haired infants.

I turn to Carol, sitting next to me and say, "That one is Jenna." "How do you know?" "I just know. I can tell." It's my first experience of mother's intuition. We are guided into the open patio area. We stand around nervously. Can we take pictures? Better not. The director of the orphanage and workers bustle about. Toddlers in plastic sandals run around laughing and stare at us. They come up and give us hugs. They hold up their arms to be lifted up. We don't know what to do. What is appropriate? Their voices echo off the concrete walls as they race in and out of the room. The nurses hand the babies to the foster parents who are standing behind the red velvet couch.

I see Jenna's foster mother start to cry as she cradles sleeping Jenna. Her husband looks down and smiles at her. I don't notice the others because I am sure I have identified the right baby. And I am correct.

In slow motion the foster mom comes up to me and hands me my bundle. She recognizes me from the picture on my application. Jenna remains asleep. I kiss her sweaty little forehead. Her chubby arms are limp on her tummy. Her black hair sticks straight up. Someone snaps a picture. A translator appears and tells me that Jenna's foster parents have bought Jenna the yellow romper outfit she is wearing with their own money. Her orange socks are held up with elastic bands. The yellow cotton romper has musical notes on it. The interpreter tells me that Jenna loves to be sung to. I thank them, trying to look them in the eyes without crying.

I have waited to be a mom forever. The foster mom wants Jenna back. She takes her and tells the interpreter what a good baby she is. Jenna cries at night, the foster dad volunteers, and loves her formula. I nod and tell the interpreter to tell them I will take such good care of her. We take pictures together. It is hard to smile at the camera and not weep at the emotion I see on the foster mom's face. Her tears stream down her face as the baby sleeps.

I see that the other adoptive moms and Todd have their babies. I fish in my backpack and hand the foster parents some gifts that we were told to bring, a book about Newburyport, handkerchiefs, things made in the USA. They seem like meaningless gifts now. Looking back, I suspect they would have liked a few hundred dollars, but we were told not to give cash. We ask if we can have the address of our foster parents. Director Li pretends she has not heard this request. She motions to bring the babies with us and come into another room for lunch. The foster mom does not want to let go of Jenna. I tell her through the interpreter that she should hold her while I'm at lunch. I will be back. The orphanage director looks disapprovingly at me.

The new parents balance their squalling babies on their laps as we eat some meat and rice around the small wooden table. The orphanage director, Director Li, is not drenched in sweat like we are. I have not seen a Chinese person sweat yet. The women wear panty hose, and polyester dresses, but appear cool as cucumbers in the stifling humidity and heat.

As we finish and go back into the main room, the orphanage director yells at Jenna's foster mom harshly. She tearfully hands Jenna back to me. Jenna can sleep through anything. Maybe it is a defense to yet another change of hands, from birth mother to police officer to orphanage workers to foster mother to nurses, back to foster mother, and now to me. She is three months old.

As I head towards the bus, the foster mom grabs Jenna one more time and leans her sideways over a bush and makes a "sssssss" sound. Jenna pees on command. The foster mom replaces her drapery fabric diaper and attaches it to her body with a thick rubber band. I stare in awe.

I hug the foster mom, who is weeping. I gently take Jenna in my arms. Someone hands me a note. My baby goes back to sleep immediately and sleeps all the way back to our guesthouse.

I cannot look back.

To Ni Gui

Dear Sara,

One time you told me that you had no memory of our first two weeks together. I will never forget that time, so I thought I'd share my memories with you. Then you can imagine, if not remember.

Love,
Mom

February 16th, 1998.

Hangzhou, China resembled Florida, with palm trees and wide-leafed bromeliads. The temperature, a warmish 45 degrees. How great to be landing in mild February vs. the sultry summer.

The swanky Mercedes bus that greeted us at the airport loaded all 12 families quickly. Our interpreter, Rose, microphone in hand, spoke English fluently. She'd be with us every day for two weeks while we finalized our adoptions: going to embassies, clinics, and municipal offices to gather needed paperwork. She had energy to spare, as she commented, with great enthusiasm on the history of the sights we passed. She even tried teaching us a Chinese lullaby, preparing us for our next task. She calmed anxieties by reporting that a Chinese pediatrician, who spoke English, had been hired by the adoption agency to stay with us in the hotel and monitor the health of the "babies."

At first, these modern amenities grated on me. I wanted my fellow adopters to have to rough it, like my first adoption trip, six years before. Searching for water, staying a month, no phones, searching for medical care at the local hospital.

Having an interpreter with us full time and a pediatrician felt like a gift, not the Herculean task our group of adoptive parents endured the time before. *They thought the time change killed them, they should have seen...* no never mind, not the time for belittling comparisons that no one on this bus cared about. I forced myself to concentrate on NOW... the crystal blue lakes we passed, the lack of smog, the high octave of horns honking.

Driving was "newish" for the general public since only the military drove in China in 1992 when Jenna came home. The car horns held a particular interest for Chinese drivers, who honked incessantly, even if stopped at a red light. The timber of the horns spoke to my nervous psyche. "Oh, yes, I am really back in China now."

Rose announced we'd "receive" the babies in the hotel at dinnertime. Cheers erupted throughout the bus from the parents to-be with anticipation. We'd not be travelling to the orphanages in person. There'd been negative tv news reports in America and Great Britain about Chinese orphanages. The BBC called the orphanages "the dying rooms." And ever since, Chinese officials refused to let adoptive parents inside orphanage gates.

Chinese adoptions had been halted for a year after that tv documentary. Our completed adoption paperwork sat in Beijing for a year and a half. We had no idea when or if we'd be matched with a child. After adoptions opened up again, I got the call on December 23th, 1997.

Ni Gui, almost two, YOU, our match. We gave you the American name Sara, easy to spell and sounded okay with Cook. We kept Gui as your middle name. That year Christmas came early.

For all but two of us on the trip, these children would be their first. My throat tightened. How can I ever really be prepared for you? Everyone else seemed giddy with excitement. Two weeks loomed large. A long time travelling solo with a toddler.

I didn't want to traumatize you more than you'd already been in your two short years. I took deep breaths. I only "knew" you through the picture that came with your referral. Jenna had deemed you "adorable," and Carol and I agreed. Shaved head and wearing a lime green hand-knit sweater. Looking like you'd been crying. Knowing you now, I bet you let it be known you didn't like holding still to have your picture taken.

What if you screamed the entire two weeks? I'd heard horror stories like that. There'd be no one else with me to trade off, or to help me gather my thoughts.

I checked my camera to make sure I had pictures left on the roll. I asked one of the dads, Pete, if he'd take our picture when the time came to meet you. Rose said it should be alphabetical so I'd be one of the first.

As we approached the hotel, the red and yellow Chinese flag danced in the breeze on the massive flagpole. We could easily have been in Boston or NYC. The hotel, so modern, unlike the primitive guesthouse six years ago in Wuhan. Easier living conditions would help me concentrate on you. No searching for a hot water spigot or food. Three restaurants in this hotel, two gift shops, a 7-11 type store, a laundry service, and working elevators, with the day of the week written on the carpet floor. No worries about running out of diapers or snacks. How did China become so modern in six years?

My room, across from Patti's on the window side, showcased the bustling traffic outdoors. She and I were adopting you and Kim, both 2-year-olds. The other adopters' babies were younger, infants, a year old. All girls.

How strange that Patti and I lived a few blocks from each other in Amesbury, MA. We each had female partners. I saw her one day in the local fish market. Somehow we got on the topic of second adoptions. I knew she had Kerri, two years younger than Jenna. In the small-world department, we discovered we were both using the same agency, both had our paperwork in, and both were waiting for a referral. We vowed to keep each other in the loop.

Our referrals came on the same day. We'd be travelling together. Neither of us revealed our living situations to the others on the trip. Our mutual social worker said to keep our partners' genders private. So I presented myself as a single mother. It was 1998.

Opening the picture window curtains wide, I gazed at rows of workers below, riding their bikes home in the rainy mist. Bright yellow, green, and red ponchos passed by with ringing bells. Bikes dodged cars, as they maneuvered through the congested traffic. Bike riders, riding two and three abreast in the street, still outnumbered the cars.

Rose popped into my room and apologized. The hotel had just run out of cribs. They promised to deliver two cushioned armchairs and extra puffs. Full of anticipatory energy, she ran back out.

I decided I'd put the chairs right up against my bed facing each other. I'd hold your hand at night if you wanted me to. No crib bars to scare you. The makeshift bed turned out to be just big enough for your compact little body. Snug as a bug. Surrounded by cozy white quilts.

Suddenly Rose ran down the hall, clipboard in hand and announced that we should all stay in our rooms. The babies had arrived. The caretakers carried all of you to the common room quietly, no onlookers allowed. I teared up.

The upheaval you all were about to experience made my stomach lurch. I peeked out my window. The huge orphanage van sat, doors opened, in the driveway, in front of the hotel. The caretakers tenderly lifted out 13 little ones all dressed in yellow snowsuits. All with your own caregivers. You looked like little ducklings from the height of my room.

I stepped away from the window to give all of you your last bit of privacy. Your last moments to understand the language spoken to you. I imagined your confusion and terror as the caretakers tell you you're meeting your new mamas. What can that mean to you?

The three-hour ride from the orphanage, so long for toddlers and infants. You all looked like you had just woken up from naps, dazed and red-cheeked.

We gathered apprehensively into a big hallway across from the conference room. The screaming and wailing behind the ornate double doors told us you were as anxious as we were. Several adoptive moms immediately began crying. My hands turned suddenly freezing cold, and my heart began pounding. I couldn't swallow. *What have I done? Here I am. Okay, stay calm. Jenna is doing well, we'll try just as hard with you.*

An orphanage worker peeked out of the double doors and smiled so sweetly. I prayed that I'd comfort you and not frighten you to death. The doors swung open and Rose announced, "Ni Gui." And there you were.

I walked over to meet you as your caregiver held you tight. You clung to a clementine in one hand and an almond cookie in the other. The caretaker bounced you up and down to encourage any facial expression. But you looked stunned with your little pouty face and pompom hat perched on the top of your shaved head. You had a red dot on your forehead to connote luck. It must have been so hot in that snowsuit and knitted hat and God knows how many layers underneath.

I smiled at you shyly. I knew to be very quiet so as not to startle you anymore than you already were. I held my breath. Your caretaker, with a big grin, put you in my arms. I almost felt guilty that I had the privilege of holding you. You looked down, no eye contact, but you didn't cry either. I whispered quietly, "Everything will be okay." I hoped my tone, if not my language, would send you the message that I loved you already.

Phil took our picture with your caretaker, and you and I were ushered quickly into the cavernous meeting room. One by one the caregivers matched the other babies with their new parents. I sat on a cushioned chair holding you sidesaddle, so you weren't forced to stare at my blonde hair and Caucasian face. I continued to whisper in your ear that you were safe.

You didn't want the cookie and orange anymore. You dropped those props to the floor. I put them in my pocket for later.

As the other babies entered with their new parents, they shrieked in terror, wept with snot coming down their noses and sucked their fingers desperately. So painful to watch, I wanted to sob. Their new parents looked as distraught as the babies. Who knows how to comfort in this tumultuous situation?

I kept patting your little thigh. I took off your woolen hat to keep you from totally overheating. I planted little, soft kisses on your shaved, sweaty head. I unzipped your yellow ducky jacket. I felt the layer upon layer of clothing underneath. I couldn't offend the caregivers by taking off your quilted snow pants. In China, the worst offense is not keeping a baby warm.

Your caregiver presented me with a picture of all the caregivers in the orphanage, like a school class picture. The orphanage director hadn't come on this trip. I'd meet her tomorrow at the Civil Affairs Bureau.

Did I have any questions about you for your caregiver? Rose asked. She'd translate for me. Too many to list, but I asked her about your favorite foods. She laughingly remarked that you ate anything. A good omen for our family. Then she volunteered that you knew your nursery rhymes and the alphabet, and you were toilet trained. She also said you walked.

As I tried to put you down to walk out with me, you quickly lifted your feet up and collapsed on the carpet. I picked you right up. I was impressed by your body language message. I get it, I'm going nowhere without you. And you're going nowhere without me. Trust me.

As I headed out the door with you in my arms, you began to whimper. I predicted full-blown screams might come next, but you waited until we were back in the States to show your full wrath, grief, and confusion. In China, you were the bravest stoic warrior.

I talked to you as I unlocked our hotel room. I only knew *ni hao*, badly pronounced, in Chinese. I had tried to learn Mandarin on Saturdays when Jenna attended Chinese dancing class. But I just couldn't get the tones, and embarrassingly, my memory would not hold onto the new phrases from week to week.

So I bantered in English. "Here we are. This is our cozy room. Wait until you see the view." Laying you down on the double bed I gently took off your snow pants and ducky jacket. The orphanage needed these back for the next group of babies. They couldn't afford to dress all of you like this each time a group met their new families. I slid off your pants, shirt and socks, parka, snow pants and hat. I packed them in a bag to return, along with a duffel bag of homemade polar fleece hats Carol made to donate to the orphanage. Orphanages had no heat in the winter.

I marveled that my long quest to adopt again had finally brought us together. I prayed to do you justice. I silently promised your parents, wherever they might be, that I'd take good care of you forever.

I kept on your pink orphanage undershirt so you had that familiar smell next to you. I remembered that orphanage musty smell from Jenna's first clothes. I hoped it comforted you in a tiny way. You had a cloth diaper on, but I put you in a Pampers. Not ready to test out the toilet-trained theory yet. You'd been sitting on a white metal enamel pot, no doubt, close to the ground, at the orphanage, not a western toilet in a swanky hotel.

You side-eyed me with no expression. I tried not to convey the uncertainty I felt at that moment. Starting from scratch again, 48 years old, this time with a toddler. But I reminded myself your birthday,

January 25th, was two days after mine. Our first connection. Very auspicious.

I dressed you in a flowered turtleneck, blue fleece sweatpants, a little knitted red vest, and winter socks. I talked to you, as you slipped into your new Tide-bleached clothes.

Next I ordered your dinner from room service. Thank goodness they spoke English. I carried you around the room as we waited for our order of pork dumplings. We looked out the window together. I showed you how the water faucets worked in the ultramodern bathroom. You weren't in the mood to put your finger in the water running out of the faucet yet. I showed you the warm water heater. You look interested in the massive bag of Cheerios on the counter I'd brought from home. I handed you a few. You had a great pincer grasp, as you popped them into your mouth. Relief washed over me. You were not too traumatized to eat.

With a knock on our door, our dinner arrived. I sat on the floor and fed you with chopsticks. You had a serious, scowling expression and looked down, but opened your mouth wide. I put a dumpling right in. "Mmmm ...was that good? You're hungry." You looked up and opened your mouth again. Eight times. Eight dumplings. I handed you a sippy cup of water. Our first meal.

I sat you down on my bed while I cleaned up from our picnic. I offered you a puppy board book. You sat motionless, staring straight ahead. When I first received your referral, I wondered how a 2-year-old would respond to new surroundings versus an infant. Often infants in this stressful experience slept poorly and wailed when awake. What would you do? I had read *Adopting the Toddler* and talked to parents who had already returned home with toddlers. New territory.

You were a tiny 12 pounds, ribs showing and undernourished. But something about your demeanor told me you were a gutsy one. You did not seem to have the same terror the year-old babies had. No temper tantrums, no screaming in the night, a huge appetite. Time would tell.

I was always consciously in awe of your courage.

Rose rushed in and said we'd have a group meeting in a few minutes. She told me to just put you to bed, keep the door open and come. She had to be kidding.

I nodded, but I knew I wouldn't put you to bed and leave the room. I'd never do that to a 2-year-old who had just met a stranger in a snazzy hotel room. I couldn't do that, period. I also knew not to debate with Rose, just find my own solution and go for it. This I had learned from trip number one to adopt Jenna. Ask permission, never granted. Just do it and smile cluelessly.

So I pulled out some purple footie pajamas from the suitcase. I checked your diaper and you were still dry. Into those jammies you went, arm-by-arm, leg by leg. Zipped up safe and sound. I carried you into the bathroom and washed your hands and face with a warm facecloth, while you sat on the counter. You stared at me. Straight on. Not a glassy stare. Real eye contact. A softening in your tender, brown eyes. I felt honored.

I quickly called home with you still in my arms. Jenna answered. When she heard my voice, she cried. Then I cried, too. She announced she'd lost another tooth in Kindergarten that day. I told her I had you in my arms. She wanted to know if you were cute. Very, I said, and brave. Carol got on the phone and I cried again. I felt so far away. Carol and Jenna were finishing breakfast, while we were cleaning up from our dinner picnic.

When Jenna said, "Bye, Mommy," she sounded younger than 6.

And you and I headed down the hall to our first group meeting. Your tiny self fit perfectly in the baby carrier on my back. I handed you a salty pretzel rod, and you grabbed it.

You didn't make a peep during the meeting. I took notes on the next day's itinerary. You and I formed our own team.

Smiles came the next day, after breakfast, when I sat you on my bed. While folding clothes, I grabbed a small terry cloth bunny from the suitcase and tossed it to you. A guttural laugh popped right out of your mouth. Ah, you had a sense of humor. I waited. You threw it back to me. And we both laughed. We had our new game.

I stopped holding my breath so much. We began to get in a travelling rhythm. You loved sitting on the bus on my back as we drove to our next appointment or walked to a shoe store to find shoes that fit your petite feet. You took in the city action as we did our errands.

You started giving me hints about you. Lover of bacon, dumplings, and noodles. Not so big on tub baths; sponge baths on the counter were safer for now. So smart. I mean how could you learn to say "mmmmm" and "more" so quickly (day 3) when the elevator opened to the dining room on the first floor? Going through the buffet line, you waited in your high chair, never a whimper. I waved to you and raised a finger to tell you I'd be right back with your feast. You followed me with your eyes.

We become a team. Attached at the hip or in the baby carrier. I'd go nowhere without you.

That's a promise.

IN GRATITUDE TO MY FEET

My pain and embarrassment were real. But they just turned a deaf ear and trudged on.

They not only learned to walk but to ride a bike without training wheels. They didn't object when I jumped off from the swing set to see how far I could fly. They got used to me hanging upside down on the jungle gym with casts on. My feet walked with me to Kindergarten and beyond. They were never late to school. They weren't so good at Duck, Duck, Goose, but they and my strong shoulders were killers at breaking through in Red Rover. At camp my feet did not know how to waterski, but they knew how to tumble on mats for the talent show.

They never said, "Don't do that, it is too risky." They were up for anything or at least gave it a go.

I kept making it more challenging for them. They tried to grip the inside of my shoes when I walked in my first pair of slippery panty hose. When I had to portage a canoe for a trip down the Sebago, they walked through the woods in flip-flops. In high school they trudged up and down the halls of Needham High and never missed a day. They were only a little annoyed as I tried to hide them by dragging my sweater in front of me. They marched in the band on Memorial Day in white bucks with no orthotics. They felt the blazing sun on their soles but kept walking to the cemetery. They put up with bandages on toes, on foot beds, on the backs of shoes to keep the non-heels from chafing and blistering.

The feet conquered driving a stick shift. One foot learned to use the clutch and gently let it out. The other learned to give the car gas and use the brake in tandem with the clutch. They drove to Illinois in one day and cross-country to California, never pooling or cramping.

They carried heavy suitcases, trunks, mini freezers, chairs, and desks, as I moved from apartment to apartment and finally to my first house. They never asked for Tylenol. Even though none was offered.

They stayed with me when I was dateless and distraught. They accompanied me each Friday as I drove to Needham to care for my ill mother. They mowed the lawn, shoveled the snow, carried railroad ties to make a border, took out the garbage, planted grass seed, and resurfaced the driveway in Newburyport. It was part of home ownership.

They never complained about shoes with not enough support or too much length to make up for the width they needed.

They took the bus with me on too many field trips to count. The State House, Boston Common, Stoneham Zoo, the butterfly museum, Harvard Museum of Natural History, Children's Museum, MFA, Peabody Essex, Ipswich River Wildlife Sanctuary, Plum Island, Lowell Theatre, Boston Symphony. For 14 years they never minded the line of children following them.

They heard themselves called "error" or "deformed". They never held it against me. They'd lay there with me while I prayed that they change into perfect feet. They only quietly rebelled by not changing one iota. They put up with comparisons. I told the doctor the right one was worse. And yet, in surgery he did the left one first. They had no say in the correction.

They had to give in to the knife, the drill, and fiberglass, but still they were with me all the way.

They mended from the staples, stitches, incisions, and skin graft. They learned to bend and walk in new ways. They welcomed the heels with open arms. They appreciated the support of the braces, crutches, and cane. They loved the TENS machine at PT when they needed a reprieve from all that new conditioning.

They were happy to get back to the classroom. They were grateful to have icepacks, pills and elevation after long days. They heard me compliment their new improved shape. They were only a little offended when I called them "my new feet."

They loved going to China and being the first to meet Jenna and Sara. It took decades to appreciate the companionship of my feet.

They were a great team. A for effort.

PART VII

EPILOGUE

Sometimes a mind is just born late, coming through waves on a slower journey.
You were never in the end alone.
Isn't it a blessing, what becomes from inside the alone.

Lidia Yuknavitch

If the body is the temple, then my outside structure was now complete. But the physical and spiritual/emotional work had just begun. The internal struggle to rebuild and feel alive and worthy was precarious. I've needed Prozac and years of therapy to buttress my delicate foundation. Often I doubted my worth and my fight for life.

I had two choices. I could give up trying to build new scaffolding with new friends, new beliefs, and new patterns of living. My other choice was to build a new structure based on my new body and growing psychological health. I am grateful I have not been pulled permanently into the riptide.

Each time I've made it back to the light.

The dark feeling I had was intense grief. I longed to have my mom see these miraculous appendages. But she was not alive. Ironically, if my mom had not died, I would not have been impelled to look for a different method of healing. She gave birth to me, and then rebirth through her death.

With her destruction came my eventual reconstruction.

To see my family would have brought Mom great joy. She had a wedding gown fund for me when I was growing up. I felt the pressure knowing interest was accruing.

But I didn't need a gown. I needed straight feet, and a new sense of confidence. I needed to figure out what I believed. I needed freedom and creativity in my life. I was done following my religion's rules and expectations It's been a fight to see myself as worthy after all those years of feeling unworthy and desperate.

Finally I built my own family, step by straight step. Carol, Jenna, and Sara showed me what a family is. They were worth the wait.

The three of them fulfilled my dream of children and companionship, something I'd never have done without the awakening I experienced from the death of my mom, and the birth of Matthew.

What I Wish I'd Known

What I Wish I'd Known…
I'm allowed to reject what I don't believe.
My voice speaks. Don't be so shy.
Trust your gut. Keep learning without apology.

What I Wish I'd Known…
Trust your intuition and find a humble doctor.
Walking straight is possible.
There are multitudes of healing modalities.

What I Wish I'd Known…
What makes *you* happy?
A valid question.
Ask it.

What I Wish I'd Known…
If intuitive non-family members want to help you,
breathe and let them.
You don't have to feel like you're continuously smothered under a
wool blanket.

What I Wish I'd Known…
Fascinating biology. Another science to study.
The fluidity of gender identification.
The shamelessness of sexual orientation.

On the other hand,
Who knows what I'd have done with all that KNOWING any earlier…

If I hadn't had to recreate my life centimeter by centimeter,
crawling through the desert,
sweating and fretting,
bleeding and weeping,

I'd never have met my numerous,
Numinous guardian angels.

*Be patient toward all that is unsolved in your heart and
try to love the questions themselves...
Live the questions now. Perhaps you will then gradually, without noticing it,
live along some distant day into the answer.*

Rainer Maria Rilke

PART VIII

END NOTES

The bold name in parentheses is the chapter where the quote was used.

(Dedication)
- Eger, E. *The Choice: Embrace the Possible.* NYC: Scribner, 2018:275.

(Captive)
- Moore, H. *The Bishop's Daughter: A Memoir.* NYC: W.W. Norton & Co., 2008:64.

(Peggy's Having Trouble)
- Hillman, J. *The Soul's Code: In Search of Character and Calling.* NYC: Ballantine Books, 2017:206.

(Silenced)
- Murdock, M. *The Heroine's Journey: Woman's Quest for Wholeness.* Colorado: Shambhala Publications, Inc., 1990:81.
- Eddy, M.B. *Science and Health with Key to the Scriptures.* Boston: The Christian Science Publishing Society, 1934:393.
- Eddy, M.B. *Feed My Sheep.* Boston: Christian Science Publishing Society, 1937:304.
- *King James Bible.* London: Hendrickson Publishers, 1611: I John 4:18.

(The Axis of Family Life)
- Winterson, J. *Why Be Happy when You Can be Normal.* NYC: Grove Press, 2011:25.
- *King James Bible.* London: Hendrickson Publishers, 1611: John 8:32.
- Eddy, M. B. *Science and Health with Key to the Scriptures.* Boston: CS Publishing Soc., 1934:494.

(These Are Not My People)
- Bolen, Jean. *Crossing to Avalon: A Woman's Midlife Quest for the Sacred Feminine.* Calif: Harper San Francisco, 2004:266.

(Saturday at the Dump)
- Galeano, E. Days and Nights of Love and War. NYC, Monthly Review Press, 2000:5.

(Under the Rack)
- Williams, T. *When Women Were Birds.* NYC, Picador, 2013:61.

(Frenzy)
- Lawrence, D.H. *The Complete Poems of D.H. Lawrence:* Head of Man. NYC: Viking Press, 1967:606.

(Perfect God, Perfect Man, and the Face)
- Williams, T. *When Women Were Birds.* NYC: Picador, 2013:77.
- Eddy, M.B. *Science and Health with Key to the Scriptures.* Boston: C.S. Publishing Soc., 1937:167.

(The Architecture of Healing)
- Woodman, M. *Coming Home to Myself: Reflections for Nurturing a Woman's Body and Soul.* Berkeley, CA: Canari Press, 1998:201.

(The Chill in the Air)
- Williams, T. *The Refuge: An Unnatural History of Family and Place.* NYC: Vintage Books, 1991:286.

(Either Here or Hereafter)
- Paris, G. Pagan *Grace: Dionysos, Hermes, and Goddess Memory in Daily Life.* Thompson, CT: Spring Publications, 1990:26.
- Eddy, M.B. *Science and Health with Key to the Scriptures.* Boston: The CS Publishing Soc., 1934:401.

(Dr. Zimbler)
- Harjo, J. *Crazy Brave: A Memoir.* NYC, W.W. Norton& Co., 2012:149.

(The Fog)

- Woodman, M. *Addicted to Perfection: The Still Unravished Bride.* Toronto: Inner City Books, 1982:23.

(Scaffolding)

- Meade, M. *Fate and Destiny, The Two Agreements of the Soul.* Seattle: GreenFire Press, 2012:185.

(Bones and Soul)

- Harjo, J. *Crazy Brave: A Memoir.* NYC: W. W. Norton & Co., 2012:164.

(The Unveiling)

- Kearney, M. *Mortally Wounded: Stories of Soul Pain, Death and Healing.* New Orleans: Spring Journal, 2007:132.

(The Embolism)

- Williams, T. *When Women Were Birds.* NC: Picador, 2013:44.

(Home)

- Smith, Maggie. *Keep Moving: Notes on Loss, Creativity, and Change.* NYC: One Signal Publishers, 2020:105.

(Epilogue)

- Yuknavitch, Lidia. *Chronology of Water: A Memoir.* Portland, Oregon: Hawthorne Books and Literary Arts, 2010: 205.
- Rilke, R.M. *Letters to a Young Poet,* translated by M.D. Herter. NYC: W.W. Norton & Co., 1993:35.

ACKNOWLEDGMENTS

Thank you to David and Linda Cook, who welcomed me into their home to recuperate from clubfeet surgery. Without their help I could never have made the commitment to seek medical care. They took me to appointments, fed me, visited me, supported me, and encouraged me throughout this process without judgment.

Thank you to Matthew Cook for being my inspiration.

Thanks goes to Dr. Seymour Zimbler for his expertise and most amazing moral support. He knew that at age 37, having clubfeet surgery was a huge undertaking. Yet he encouraged me and patiently explained every procedure. His compassion and tenderness will never be forgotten. He will always be my father figure.

Thanks also goes to Newton Wellesley Hospital for their careful care and understanding with a very frightened patient.

Special thanks goes to my wonderful friend, Sherry Moore, for visiting me every weekend during this process. She brought laughs, news, and compassion. She sat with me while I learned how to drive again with my new heels. She took me to doctor appointments, shopped for ugly shoes with me, and generally kept me sane. Friends like her do not come around often.

Thanks to Sue Harbour who encouraged me to be a "person" to come out of my shell and express what I was feeling. Thanks to her for those important discussions on our rides to school.

Thanks, and all my love to my mom for my birth and rebirth. She's my prime example of what real courage is. She showed me unwavering love even when I was an angry, rude daughter. She showed me the importance of self-love and care.

I thank my partner, Carol, and my children, Jenna and Sara, for encouraging me to write this down if only for myself. The three of them gave me joy I never experienced before. A chance to build a family is the best gift.

I thank Joseph Connelly, the Superintendent of the Boxford Public Schools at the time, for giving me medical leave and then adoption leave with such support. And to Nancy Diamonti, the Principal, who was so flexible when I returned to teach with all kinds of orthopedic paraphernalia.

My writing course at Pacifica Graduate Institute in Santa Barbara, California, gave me the space to share my writing for the first time with others besides my therapist. I had never had so many positive affirmations before in the truth of my story. The course showed me I DID have the words. Special gratitude to my ever-supportive writing teacher, Jennifer Leigh Selig, PhD., and to my writing companions in the Writing Down the Soul courses.

Deepest thanks to my therapist, Dr. Christine Flaherty, PhD., for so much. Thanks to her for encouraging me to express myself, first with art. She waited patiently for the words. The images flowed. She allowed me to share these with her and puzzle out their meanings. She taught me what I felt was real. My art helped heal my fear of verbal expression. The act of making art helped me come to terms with what I had seen. My lost words then re-emerged. We were on a life-saving mission together.

How can you thank someone enough for a life rebuilt? For a life saved?

Made in the USA
Las Vegas, NV
29 December 2021

39742686R00142